Prof. Simmy Smith

D1442325

THE DOCTOR WHO
WHO
ILLUSTRATED A-Z

THE DOCTOR WHO
ILLUSTRATED A-Z

LESLEY STANDRING

W.H. ALLEN · LONDON
1985

To my mum for typing out the manuscript
and surviving Longleat

Illustrations and text copyright © Lesley Standing, 1985

'Doctor Who' series copyright © British Broadcasting Corporation, 1985

Typesetting and origination by Avocet, Aylesbury, Bucks
Printed and bound in Great Britain by
Anchor Brendon Ltd, Tiptree, Essex
for the Publishers, W.H. Allen & Co. PLC
44 Hill Street, London W1X 8LB

ISBN 0 491 03484 9

A

ABOMINABLE SNOWMAN

See *Yeti*

ADRASTA

The tyranical ruler of Chloris, a planet scarce in minerals. Her power derived from her monopoly of all metals on the planet which she dominated by means of vicious wolf-weed guard dogs. She was eventually killed by Erato.

THE CREATURE FROM THE PIT
See also *Erato*

ADRIC

A young Alzarian who stowed away on the TARDIS. He was a mathematically gifted companion, though prone to a lack of common sense which often caused problems for both himself and the Doctor. He died heroically, opposing the Cybermen in a futile attempt to save the Earth from collision with a bomb-laden freighter.

FULL CIRCLE – EARTHSHOCK
See also *Alzarius*

AGGEDOR

A semi-mythical sacred beast of the planet Peladon. He was used by the unscrupulous high priest Hepesh to destroy his enemies, but was tamed by the Doctor. Aggedor was killed by Eckersley who died himself in the struggle.

THE CURSE OF PELADON
THE MONSTER OF PELADON
See also *Eckersley, Hepesh, Peladon*

ALPHA CENTAURI
Timid six-limbed being of the planet Alpha Centauri. An Ambassador for the Federation, he aided the Doctor on both his visits to Peladon.

THE CURSE OF PELADON
THE MONSTER OF PELADON
See also *Peladon*

ALYDON
The Thal leader who succeeded Temmosus after the latter's murder by the Daleks.

THE DEAD PLANET
See also *Thals*

ALZARIUS
At mistfall the inhabitants of the planet Alzarius resume a rapid evolutionary cycle, from spiders to marshmen to humans. The humans, unaware of their ancestry, inhabit a crashed spaceship, the Starliner, believing themselves to be descendants of the long-dead passengers from Terradon.

FULL CIRCLE
See also *Starliner*

AMBOISE, ABBOT OF
A French catholic and double of the first Doctor. He was murdered before the St Bartholomew's Day massacre.

THE MASSACRE

AMDO
The goddess of the fishpeople of Atlantis who was impersonated by Polly.

THE UNDERWATER MENACE

ANDRED
The commander of the Chancellery guard which protects the Capitol on Gallifrey. Leela chose to remain with Andred after the defeat of the Sontaran invaders.

THE INVASION OF TIME

ANDROIDS

Sophisticated robots often indistinguishable from human beings. The Doctor has encountered various types of androids on his travels, memorable examples of which include the Movellans, the Androids of Tara, the Terileptil robot, Monarch's army of ethnic androids from Earth and a one time TARDIS crewmember, Kamelion. The Doctor has also been confronted by android replicas of himself, the first created by the Daleks, the other by the Kraals.

ANDROZANI (MAJOR AND MINOR)

Androzani's two planets were dominated by the Spectrox conglomerate. Major, the administrative centre, faced political turmoil due to the severance of their Spectrox supplies by Sharaz Jek on Minor. Minor was inhospitable, prone to mud-bursts and marauding carnivores, but housed the valuable raw Spectrox.

THE CAVES OF ANDROZANI
See also *Sharaz Jek, Morgus, Spectrox*

ANETH

A peaceful planet which was forced to provide sacrifices of youths, maidens and Hymetusite to the Nimon.

THE HORNS OF NIMON

ANIMUS

Crouched at the centre of its web on Vortis the Animus controlled the minds of the Zarbi and of the Doctor's companions by means of ornaments made of gold. Barbara destroyed it with a cell destructor gun as it attempted to absorb the Doctor and Vicki.

THE WEB PLANET
See also *Vortis, Zarbi*

ANTI-MATTER

The opposite of matter. It exists in an anti-matter universe parallel to our own and is deadly to anything which is not itself constructed of anti-matter.

ANTI-MATTER MONSTER

A mysterious being found on the planet Zeta Minor. It attacked a Morestran survey team when one of the members, Professor Sorenson, attempted to remove anti-matter from the planet.

PLANET OF EVIL
See also *Sorenson*

APC NET

The Amplified Panatropic Computations form part of the Matrix which contains the brain cells of every dead Time Lord. The Doctor made a mental journey into the Matrix where he was almost destroyed by the Master.

THE DEADLY ASSASSIN

ARAK

The leader of the human slaves of the planet Metebelis Three who revolted and defeated their spider overlords.

PLANET OF THE SPIDERS

ARBITAN

The keeper of the Conscience of Marinus.

Arbitan forced the Doctor and his companions to search for the four keys to the conscience; in their absence he was killed by the Voord.

THE KEYS OF MARINUS
See also *Conscience, Voord*

ARCTURUS
A delegate of the Federation confined within a life support system, Arcturus conspired to prevent Peladon's admission to the Federation.

THE CURSE OF PELADON
See also *Aggedor, Alpha Centauri, Ice Warriors*

ARGOLIS
The planet of the Argolin, creators of the Leisure Hive. The planet was devastated and the Argolins made sterile by a nuclear war with the Foamasi. The race survived by means of the Tachyon Generator.

THE LEISURE HIVE
See also *Foamasi*

ARGONITE
An extremely precious metal sought by the space pirate Caven.

THE SPACE PIRATES

ARIDIUS
A desert planet populated by half-human, half-amphibian Aridians and their flesh-eating enemies, the Mire Beasts. The deadliest danger of Aridius, however, proved to be the Daleks in pursuit of the Doctor.

THE CHASE

ARIS
A member of the peaceful Kinda, Aris was temporarily taken over by the Mara.

KINDA

ARK
Populated by humans and their Monoid slaves, the Ark was a vast spaceship transporting the seeds of humanity to a new beginning on the planet Refusis. En route, the Monoids became the masters, almost destroying the Ark.

THE ARK

ARK

See *Nerva*

ASTRA
Princess Astra of Atrios proved to be the final segment of the Key to Time. When the Doctor dispersed the Key, Astra was returned to her rightful position in time and space.

THE ARMAGEDDON FACTOR
See also *Romana*

ASTRAL MAP
An instrument in the TARDIS which was used by the Animus to locate the Menoptera invasion force.

THE WEB PLANET

ASTRID
The assistant of Giles Kent who, unaware of his ruthless ambition, helped him and the Doctor to defeat Salamander.

ENEMY OF THE WORLD

ATLANTIS
Prominent in Earth legends, Atlantis was visited by the Doctor on two separate occasions – to prevent the Master from using the power of Kronos, and to stop Professor Zaroff's experiments to raise the city from the sea bed. Although Azal the Daemon claimed responsibility for the destruction of Atlantis, both of the Doctor's visits also ended in its devastation.

THE UNDERWATER MENACE
THE TIME MONSTER

ATRIOS
A planet which was involved in a devastating war with its twin, Zeos. Here the Doctor and the Shadow battled to discover the final segment of the Key to Time.

THE ARMAGEDDON FACTOR
See also *Astra*

AUKON
Originally named science officer O'Connor, he and his two companions Zargo and Camilla were kidnapped in their spaceship *Hydrax* and became victims and servants of the Great Vampire. They ruled and terrorised the local community for generations until the Doctor killed the Great Vampire, thus ending their lives.

STATE OF DECAY
See also *Great Vampire*

AUTLOC
Aztec high priest of knowledge. Barbara hoped to end the practice of human sacrifice with the aid of this enlightened man.

THE AZTECS

AUTONS

The creations of the Nestenes, they were constructed from living plastic and could be virtually any shape. Examples include a doll, an armchair, a telephone line and plastic daffodils, all of which suffocated their victims; also an army of dummies equipped with deadly wrist guns.

SPEARHEAD FROM SPACE
TERROR OF THE AUTONS

AXOS

A parasitic creature which was guided to Earth by the Master. The Axons, a component part of Axos, initially assumed the form of benevolent golden beings offering Earth axonite – a substance capable of increasing or reducing matter. In reality they were tentacled monsters using axonite to drain planets of energy. The Doctor trapped Axos in a time loop.

THE CLAWS OF AXOS

AZAL

Last of the Daemons, he was accidentally revived when an ancient burial mound was opened. Azal, disappointed with the human race, was torn between destroying Earth or transferring his powers to the Doctor. Jo's act of self-sacrifice, interposing herself between the Doctor and Azal, deflected his energy, thus killing him.

THE DAEMONS
See also *Daemons, Bok*

AZTECS

A Central American civilization who worshipped and made human sacrifice to the sun.

B

BARBARA WRIGHT

A teacher of History and English at Coal Hill School, England. She and her colleague, Ian Chesterton, became the Doctor's unwilling companions when they forced their way into the TARDIS in search of a baffling pupil, Susan. After many journeys she and Ian were returned to twentieth-century England.

AN UNEARTHLY CHILD – THE CHASE

BELLAL

A kindly native of the planet Exxilon, he helped the third Doctor against the Daleks and the more belligerent members of his own race.

DEATH TO THE DALEKS

BEN JACKSON

Ben was a merchant seaman who helped the Doctor to defeat the War Machines. Accidentally entering the TARDIS with Polly, he became a companion and witnessed the first Doctor's regeneration. After his encounter with the Chameleons he chose to remain on Earth with Polly.

THE WAR MACHINES – THE FACELESS ONES

BENTON

A long-term member of UNIT, he first met the Doctor during the Cybermen invasion and has remained extremely loyal to him throughout three incarnations. Originally a corporal, he was promoted to sergeant and then RSM.

THE INVASION – THE ANDROID INVASION

BESSIE
A yellow Edwardian roadster presented to the third Doctor by the Brigadier.

SPEARHEAD FROM SPACE – THE FIVE DOCTORS

BI-AL FOUNDATION
The centre for alien biomorphology on Asteroid K4067 was a research hospital near the planet Titan where the Doctor hoped to free his mind from the influence of the Nucleus.

THE INVISIBLE ENEMY

BIGON
Originally an Athenian philosopher from planet Earth, he was kidnapped by Monarch and given immortality in the form of an android body, his humanity preserved in a microchip. He helped the Doctor to foil Monarch's plans.

FOUR TO DOOMSDAY

BIROC
A Tharil time-sensitive and captive navigator of Rorvik's slaveship, Biroc survived to lead his people to a new beginning beyond the Gateway.

WARRIORS' GATE

BLOCK TRANSFER COMPUTATIONS
The manipulation of numbers directly changing the physical world. It was practised by the mathematicians of Logopolis to contain universal entropy.

LOGOPOLIS
CASTROVALVA
See also *CVE, Logopolis*

BOK
A stone gargoyle, brought to life by Azal. Capable of flight and of delivering deadly

thunderbolts of energy from its outstretched claw, Bok proved a formidable adversary. Reverting to stone when Azal died, it smashed into pieces.

THE DAEMONS

BORUSA
A former tutor of the Doctor at the Academy, the Time Lord Borusa advanced from the position of Cardinal to Chancellor and eventually became President of the Time Lords. An enigmatic and astute politician, he was originally content to influence the High Council from behind the scenes, viewing the role of President as a mere figurehead. Perhaps presidential responsibilities changed Borusa – in protecting the Capitol from the threat of Omega he proved capable of ordering the innocent Doctor's death. Eventually, his moral judgements obscured by ambition, he broke the rules of time, endangering the lives of all five Doctors and their companions in his plan to become immortal and rule the Time Lords forever. He attained immortality, imprisoned in stone for eternity on the Tomb of Rassilon: a sad end for one who had once commanded the respect of the Time Lords, including the Doctor.

THE DEADLY ASSASSIN – THE FIVE DOCTORS

BRAZEN
The Chief Orderly on Frontios. A proficient and seasoned commander he advised and encouraged his young leader

Plantagenet. Whilst rescuing the former from the Tractators, Brazen fell victim to their excavating machine.

FRONTIOS
See also *Plantagenet, Frontios*

BOSS
The Biomorphic Organisational Systems Supervisor was the megalomaniac computer of Global Chemicals which the Doctor argued into non-existence.

THE GREEN DEATH

BRIGADIER
Alastair Gordon Lethbridge-Stewart, Commanding Officer of the British section of UNIT. A no-nonsense military man, he first met the Doctor during the Yeti invasion as a colonel and has remained a steadfast, though often bemused, friend through four of the Doctor's incarnations. Now retired, he teaches 'A' level maths at a boys' school.

THE WEB OF FEAR – THE FIVE DOCTORS

BROTON
The leader of the Zygons who impersonated the Duke of Forgill to gain admission to the International Energy Conference. He was shot by the Brigadier whilst attempting to exterminate the inhabitants of Earth.

TERROR OF THE ZYGONS
See also *Zygons*

13

CAILLEACH
A Druid goddess impersonated by Cessair of Diplos.

THE STONES OF BLOOD

CALUFRAX
The second segment of the Key to Time. This unfortunate planet was crushed to the size of a football by the Pirate Planet.

THE PIRATE PLANET

CAMECA
An Aztec lady to whom the first Doctor became unwittingly engaged.

THE AZTECS

CAMILLA
Formerly navigation officer Lauren MacMillan

STATE OF DECAY
See also *Aukon, Great Vampire, Hydrax, Zargo*

CAMPBELL, DAVID
A young member of the resistance against the Dalek invasion of Earth. Susan chose to stay behind and marry him.

THE DALEK INVASION OF EARTH

CAPTAIN
The pirate pilot of Zanak – half man, half Cyborg. He was eventually destroyed by his evil mistress, Queen Xanxia.

THE PIRATE PLANET

CARSTAIRS, LIEUTENANT
A British officer who, during the first World War, was transported without his knowledge or consent to the War Games. Discovering the deception, he helped the Doctor against the War Lord.

THE WAR GAMES

CASTROVALVA
An illusionary city created by the Block Transfer Computations of Adric whilst he was under the control of the Master.

CASTROVALVA
See also *Block Transfer Computations*

CATHERINE DE'MEDICI
The Catholic Queen who instigated the infamous St Bartholomew's Day Massacre.

THE MASSACRE

CAVEN
A murderous space pilot who plundered space beacons for argonite. He committed suicide by blowing up his ship.

THE SPACE PIRATES
See also *Argonite, Issigri*

CELESTIAL TOYMAKER
A mandarin-like character who forced his

prisoners to participate in a series of deadly games. The Doctor escaped his clutches by outwitting him in the Trilogic Game.

THE CELESTIAL TOYMAKER

CELL DESTRUCTOR GUN
It was used by Barbara to destroy the Animus on Vortis.

THE WEB PLANET

CEREBRATION MENTOR
A machine designed by Tobias Vaughn which was capable of generating emotional impulses. It proved effective on both humans and Cybermen.

THE INVASION

CESSAIR OF DIPLOS
A female criminal who stole the seal of Diplos, one of the segments of the Key to Time. She was hunted down and sentenced to perpetual imprisonment by the Megara.

THE STONES OF BLOOD
See also *Cailleach, Megara, Vivien Fay*

CET MACHINE
The Continuous Event Transmuter, invented by Tryst, captured portions of alien planets in crystals to be projected later as a slide show. The instability induced by the materialisation of two spacecraft in the same space made it possible for Mandrels to escape from the Eden projection.

NIGHTMARE OF EDEN

CHAMELEONS
A race made homeless and faceless after a global war, they developed a process for stealing human identity as a prelude to the colonisation of Earth.

THE FACELESS ONES

CHAMELEON CIRCUIT
An instrument which enables a TARDIS to change its appearance and blend with its surroundings. Unfortunately, the Doctor's jammed when he landed in Totters Yard.

AN UNEARTHLY CHILD

CHANNING
Although human in appearance he was, in reality, an Auton. He died when the Nestene on Earth was destroyed.

SPEARHEAD FROM SPACE

CHASE, HARRISON
A maniacal millionaire whose obsession with plant life led him to steal and grow a Krynoid. He became compost after perishing in his own crushing machine.

THE SEEDS OF DOOM
See also *Krynoid*

CHELLAK, GENERAL
The commander of the Federation Troops opposing Sharaz Jek on Androzani Minor. Chellak's effectiveness was undermined by the duplicity of his superior Morgus, and compounded by the substitution of his aide Major Salateen for an android copy.

15

The ill-fated General died as a mud-burst swept the tunnels of Androzani Minor.

THE CAVES OF ANDROZANI
See also *Morgus, Salateen, Sharaz Jek*

CHEN, MAVIC
The traitorous guardian of the solar system who joined the Dalek alliance, giving them the taranium core. They eventually killed him.

THE DALEK MASTER PLAN
See also *Taranium Core*

CHLORIS
A green planet rich in chlorophyll, but devoid of metals. It is the home of the wolf-weeds.

THE CREATURE FROM THE PIT
See also *Adrasta, Erato*

CHO-JE
Tibetan monk and alternative body of K'anpo. He helped the Doctor through his traumatic third regeneration when his body was riddled with radiation.

PLANET OF THE SPIDERS
See also *Great One*

CHRONIC HYSTERESIS
A form of time loop engineered by Meglos to trap the Doctor.

MEGLOS

CHRONOTIS, PROFESSOR
The name adopted by a retired Time Lord living on Earth and teaching at Cambridge University. He possessed a valuable Gallifreyan book containing information on Shada. In reality he was Salyavin.

SHADA
See also *Salyavin, Shada*

CHUMBLIES
A name invented by Vicki to describe the nature of the robotic servants of the Rills.

GALAXY FOUR

CLANCEY, MILO
An eccentric old prospector who helped the Doctor to find the space pirates, his old friend and partner Dom Issigri and, finally, the TARDIS.

THE SPACE PIRATES
See also *LIZ 79*

CLOCKWORK SOLDIERS
These frightening, though ficticious, soldiers were mental creations of the Master of the Land of Fiction.

THE MIND ROBBER

CLOISTER BELL
A TARDIS alarm signal which is triggered only in extreme emergencies.

COMPANY
The manufacturers of the artificial suns around Pluto. The Company was a business operation which subjugates its human workers by an oppressive tax

system. It was controlled by the Usarians, but went into voluntary liquidation when it was defeated by the Doctor.

THE SUN MAKERS

CONCORDE
A type of supersonic jet used on twentieth century Earth, two of which were transported 140 million years into Earth's past by the Master.

TIME FLIGHT
See also *Captain Stapley, Kalid, Plasmatons*

CONDO
Solon's barbarian servant whose loyalty depended upon Solon's promises to restore his amputated arm. On finding his missing limb attached to the Morbius monster, Condo attacked his master who shot him. Mortally wounded, Condo expired fighting the monster.

THE BRAIN OF MORBIUS

CONSCIENCE
A giant machine which served as a conscience for the people of Marinus, preventing any evil thought. It was destroyed by a Voord.

THE KEYS OF MARINUS

CORY, MARC
Space special security agent Cory travelled to the planet Kembel where he compiled a valuable tape concerning the Dalek Masterplan. He was exterminated, but the tape survived to be found by the Doctor.

MISSION TO THE UNKNOWN

CRANLEIGH
The name of a titled English family with which the Doctor became involved. George Cranleigh, a crazy disfigured botanist, kidnapped Nyssa mistaking her for his fiancée, Ann Talbot. He plunged to his death from the rooftops.

BLACK ORCHID

CRATER OF NEEDLES
A slave colony on the planet Vortis which provided the Animus with fuel to increase its power.

THE WEB PLANET

CRINOTH
A planet which was sucked dry by the Nimon who were themselves destroyed when Crinoth exploded.

THE HORNS OF NIMON
See also *Nimon*

CULLODEN
Scene of the Scottish defeat by the English, from which Jamie and other survivors of his clan were escaping when they encountered the Doctor.

THE HIGHLANDERS

CULLY
The rebellious son of the Dulcian leader.

He and Jamie helped to defeat the Dominators.

THE DOMINATORS

CVE
The Charged Vacuum Emboitements created voids leading from one universe to another, e.g. E-Space. They were maintained by the Block Transfer Computations of Logopolis.

FULL CIRCLE – LOGOPOLIS
See also *Block Transfer Computations, Logopolis*

CYBER ANDROIDS
Deadly black androids controlled by the Cybermen. They massacred an archaelogical survey team who came too close to a hidden bomb intended to destroy the Earth.

EARTHSHOCK
See also *Cybermen*

CYBERMATS
Small, mechanical rat-like creatures used by the Cybermen. They are capable of injecting a deadly poison.

THE TOMB OF THE CYBERMEN
THE WHEEL IN SPACE
REVENGE OF THE CYBERMEN
See also *Cybermen*

CYBERMEN
Originally humans, the scientists of Mondas perfected cybernetics (the reproduction of machine functions in human beings). Initially replacing only their limbs with metal and plastic they gradually progressed to the nervous system and finally the brain. The end product was the Cybermen, formidable metallic giants, devoid of emotion, ruthlessly logical, immensely strong and intent on conquest. Their great weakness is that gold is fatal to them.

THE TENTH PLANET – ATTACK OF THE CYBERMEN
See also *Voga*

18

DAEMONS

Immensely powerful beings from the planet Damos who visited Earth and, as an experiment, assisted mankind on the path to developing intelligence. They have the ability to diminish themselves, a process which releases huge amounts of energy.

THE DAEMONS
See also *Azal*

DALEKANIUM BOMB

Dalekanium is a versatile explosive substance developed by the Daleks. It was used by human guerillas to destroy the Daleks who were attempting to change Earth's future.

DAY OF THE DALEKS

DALEKS

The Daleks are the mutated remains of the Kaled race whose true form, that of a malevolent clawed slug, is encased for protection and mobility within a metallic shell. Although intelligent, they possess no individual aspirations and are totally loyal to the Emperor Dalek and his subordinate, the Black Dalek. The name Dalek is an anagram of Kaled, the race from which they were developed by Davros to defeat the Thals and become masters of Skaro. Their ambition however proved boundless. They began to move through time and space, pitilessly exterminating all who stood in the path of their ultimate goal, total domination of the universe. This has brought them into constant conflict with the Doctor who has opposed them all his lives, and with the Movellans whose strengths and ambitions are very similar to their own.

THE DEAD PLANET – REVELATION OF THE DALEKS
See also *Davros, Kaleds, Movellans, Skaro, Thals*

DAVROS

A brilliant Kaled scientist crippled by radiation, he developed the Daleks from specially-bred mutations of the Kaled race. Devoid of pity or moral conscience he helped the Thals annihilate his own people when the future of his Daleks was threatened. Created in Davros's own ruthless image, the Daleks ultimately attempted his extermination, but lacking his creative adaptability were reluctantly compelled to revive him. Following both resurrections, Davros struggled to eliminate the Movellan threat and regain dominance over his errant creations, latterly via a Dalek virus to which he apparently, but by no means definitely, succumbed.

GENESIS OF THE DALEKS – REVELATION OF THE DALEKS
See also *Daleks, Kaleds, Movellans*

DELTA MAGNA

The Swampies' planet of origin, Delta Magna became colonised by humans who relocated the Swampies to one of its moons, Delta Three.

THE POWER OF KROLL

DELTA THREE
The home of the Swampies and their god Kroll.

THE POWER OF KROLL

DEMNOS
The cult of Demnos originated in Rome, involved human sacrifice and was believed to have died out in the third century. It survived, however, resurfacing in fifteenth century Italy where the worshippers and their leader Hieronymous were taken over by the Mandragora Helix.

THE MASQUE OF MANDRAGORA

DENT, CAPTAIN
A ruthless career man employed by IMC. He used a clawed mining robot to terrorise the colonists on Exarius into abandoning their homes.

COLONY IN SPACE
See also *Doomsday Weapon*

DEONS
The Deons formed the religious element of Tigellan society who guarded and worshipped the Dodecahedron, believing it to be a gift from the gods.

MEGLOS

DEVA LOKA
The planet of the peaceful Kinda. It was invaded by the Mara which infiltrated the Deva Lokans' minds via the Windchimes.

KINDA
See also *Mara*

DIDO
The tranquillity of the peaceful Didonians was shattered when an Earth ship bearing Vicki and Bennett crash-landed on Dido. Several Didonians died before Bennett's murderous schemes were discovered.

THE RESCUE
See also *Koquilion*

DIMENSIONALLY TRANSCENDENTAL
A term which describes the TARDIS's facility to be larger on the inside than the outside.

See also *TARDIS*

DINOSAURS
The Doctor has encountered these large prehistoric Earth crreatures on more than one occasion - Operation Golden Age transported several to twentieth century London, and the Silurians kept them as pets. The extinction of these huge beasts was apparently caused by the massive explosion which also claimed the life of Adric.

DIPLOS
The planet of Cessair, from which she stole the great seal of Diplos, in reality one

The Celestial Toymaker and his playthings, watched over by the Pirate Captain.

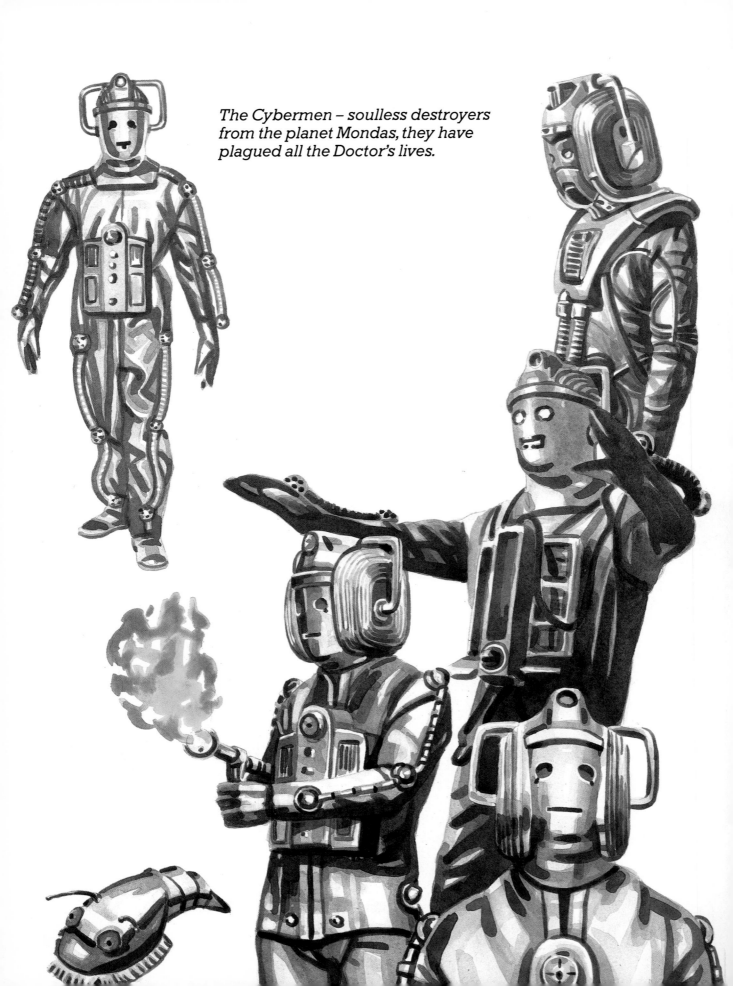

The Cybermen – soulless destroyers from the planet Mondas, they have plagued all the Doctor's lives.

The dreaded Daleks, monstrous mutations from the planet Skaro, and their evil creator Davros.

The six incarnations of the Doctor.

of the segments of the Key to Time.

THE STONES OF BLOOD
See also *Key to Time*

DISINTEGRATOR GUN
This advanced weapon was constructed
from materials stolen by the Giant Robot
who then used it to gain access to
invaluable documents relating to missile
locations. The Brigadier misguidedly fired
it at the robot, causing it to grow to an
enormous size.

ROBOT
See also *Giant Robot*

DN6
A deadly insecticide developed by
Forester which was capable of destroying
all insect life on Earth. The Doctor
destroyed it with fire, but not before it had
contaminated a miniaturised Barbara.

PLANET OF GIANTS

THE DOCTOR
An eccentrically brilliant Time Lord of the
planet Gallifrey who, bored by the
conventions and sedentary lifestyle of his
people, 'appropriated' a TARDIS and
became a traveller in time and space. Like
all Time Lords he has two hearts, a
temperature of 60° Fahrenheit and the
unnerving ability, when his body becomes
old or damaged, to regenerate into a new
one. The Doctor is now over 750 years old
and has regenerated five times, each one
introducing both personality and bodily
changes.

First Doctor
The white-haired old man known as the
first Doctor tended to be an observer, loth
to interfere with history. This, and his often
arrogant nature, occasionally led him into
conflict with his human companions, but
time mellowed his attitudes, and when he
collapsed following a confrontation with
the Cybermen he regenerated into a
humorous, eccentric little man.

21

Second Doctor

The second Doctor often hid his brilliant intellect beneath a veneer of absentminded foolery, a ploy which led his enemies to underestimate him. It was in this incarnation that the renegade Doctor was eventually captured and brought to trial by the Time Lords. His moving speech, claiming that it was their moral duty to help the weak and oppressed, ultimately influenced Time Lord policy; his life was spared, his body forcibly regenerated and exiled to Earth, and his memory of how to operate the TARDIS erased.

scientific adviser to UNIT, he foiled several alien invasions, more than one of which was instigated by his arch enemy, the Master. Following the incident in which all three Doctors combined to defeat Omega, his sentence of exile was revoked, leaving him free to resume his travels. An incident involving the spiders of Metebelis Three necessitated his third regeneration.

Third Doctor

This new Doctor, the third, with a passion for flamboyant clothes, fast vehicles and interesting gadgets, proved a heroic man of action. Consenting to act as unofficial

Fourth Doctor

The fourth Doctor, possessing many characteristics of his former selves, was often prone to stroll into potentially dangerous situations equipped with only his scarf, floppy hat, broad grin and the occasional jelly baby. His insatiable curiosity for other worlds caused him to gradually sever his connections with Earth and it was during this incarnation that he paid two reluctant visits to his home planet – Gallifrey. The first visit involved an assassination plot on the President in which he was implicated by the Master. The second, an invasion attempt by first the Vardans and then the Sontarans, to prevent which the Doctor briefly became Lord President of the Time Lords.

His fourth regeneration was precipitated by the Master who caused the Doctor to fall from a great height, fatally crushing him. Luckily the incident had been prepared for – the Watcher, the Doctor's alternative body, merged with the old one to become the fifth and youngest Doctor yet.

Fifth Doctor

Overcoming a few initial hitches with his new form the fresh-faced fifth Doctor donned Edwardian cricketing garb with a ubiquitous stick of celery pinned to his lapel. Exuding the air of an inquisitive innocent the youthful Doctor displayed limitless ingenuity in rectifying his own miscalculations and foiling the frequent manifestations of the Master. During one such encounter, the most bizarre of this incarnation, he was reunited with three of his former selves in the Death Zone on Gallifrey (the fourth Doctor being stranded in the time vortex). There he faced the legendary Rassilon. When infected by spectrox toxaemia, a terminal

disease against which even the medicinal properties of his celery proved useless, the Doctor lapsed into his fifth regeneration.

Sixth Doctor
The initial characteristics of the sixth Doctor emerging from a highly unstable regeneration proved most peculiar. He displayed arrogance, cowardice and self-pity, attempted to strangle his companion, Peri, and exhibited appalling taste in clothes. As he stabilised however these transitory features resolved themselves, but his multicoloured apparel remained.

Despite numerous regenerations certain aspects of the Doctor remain constant: his brilliant scientific mind, endearing fallibility, creative improvisation and intense sense of moral justice.

See also *Gallifrey, Master, Time Lords*

DODECAHEDRON
It was developed on Zolfa-Thura as an energy source, but its military potential was soon recognised by a section of Zolfa-Thuran society including Meglos. To prevent its misuse it was taken to Tigella where the relatively primitive natives discovered it, worshipped it and used it to power their underground city.

MEGLOS
See also *Deons, Meglos*

DODO
Dorothea Chaplet rushed into the TARDIS on her way home from school, understandably mistaking it for a police box. Despite her Cockney accent and constant use of Sixties' slang, she reminded the Doctor of Susan. She remained with the Doctor until the TARDIS finally arrived back in her own time (England 1966). An encounter with WOTAN on her return left her hypnotised for a while and she stayed in England to recover.

THE MASSACRE – THE WAR MACHINES

DOJJEN
A Manussan Director whose researches into the myths of the Mara led him to abandon his post and prepare himself through meditation to withstand the mental onslaughts of the Mara.

SNAKEDANCE

DOMINATORS
A belligerent race who, with their robot Quarks, invaded the world of the pacifist Dulcians. They planned to explode rockets and atomic seed capsules into the core of Dulkis, releasing vast levels of radiation which the Dominator space fleet would subsequently absorb as fuel. The

Doctor resituated the atomic device within the Dominator spaceship, with predictable results.

THE DOMINATORS

DOOMSDAY WEAPON
The Doomsday machine file, stolen by the Master from the Time Lords, located this devastating weapon capable of destroying worlds, on the planet Exarius. There the Doctor encountered the Guardian, last survivor of a race withered and sterilised by the fallout from the machine they safeguarded. The Doctor finally persuaded the Guardian to destroy the machine.

COLONY IN SPACE
See also *Guardian*

DRACONIANS
The Draconians, an honourable, arrogant, aristocratic race, came into conflict with Earth in the 26th Century as both empires expanded. They were sometimes referred to as 'Dragons' by Earthpeople, partly due to their green, scaly appearance, but also in memory of the bloody three day war between the two races. A second war, engineered by the Master with his Ogron servants, was narrowly averted by the Doctor.

FRONTIER IN SPACE

DRAHVINS
A vicious warrior race of beautiful cloned females led by Maaga. They attempted to escape from the doomed planet in Galaxy Four on which they had crashlanded by stealing the ship of the pacifist Rills. The Doctor wasn't deceived by their protestations of innocence and when the planet exploded it was the Drahvins who perished.

GALAXY FOUR

DRASHIGS
Fearsome carnivorous monsters occupying a swampland within the Scope. One escaped from its alloted area,

25

pursued Jo and the Doctor and eventually emerged and swallowed a devious saboteur. The remaining Drashigs were returned to their planet of origin.

CARNIVAL OF MONSTERS
See also *Scope*

DRAX
An itinerant Time Lord of dubious character who built the Mentalis Computer on Zeos and consented to use his talents to help the Doctor defeat the Shadow. Drax had acquired a broad Cockney accent whilst serving a ten year sentence in Brixton prison in London.

THE ARMAGEDDON FACTOR

DUGGAN
An inept English detective whose subtle tactics of hitting suspects over the head at the first possible opportunity helped and hindered the Doctor's investigations of Scaroth and the Paris time disturbances,

CITY OF DEATH

DUKKHA
A malevolently devious manifestation of the Mara whom Tegan encountered in her inner mind whilst dreaming beneath the wind-chimes. The Mara passed via Dukkha to Tegan and thence to Aris.

KINDA
See also *Mara*

DULKIS
The Dulcians, pacifist inhabitants of the planet Dulkis, had banned the use of weapons and built a museum to remind people of the horror of war. The ruthless Dominators attempted to reduce Dulkis to a radioactive mass.

THE DOMINATORS
See also *Dominators, Quarks*

DWARF STAR ALLOY
An incredibly heavy and expensive metal which is formed by the compaction of a sun collapsing in on itself. Rorvik's spaceship was constructed of the alloy as it is the only substance capable of restraining the time-sensitive Tharils.

WARRIORS' GATE
See also *Tharils*

DYNATROPE
The Dynatrope absorbed intelligence and used it as an energy source to awaken the sleeping Krotons. The minds of Zoe and the Doctor unwittingly supplied the energy required to begin the re-animation, but discovering that the Dynatrope was made of tellurium the Doctor was able to destroy it with a sulphuric acid solution.

THE KROTONS
See also *Krotons*

EARP, WYATT
Wyatt Earp, the notorious gunfighting lawman, his two brothers Warren and Virgil and their friend Doc Holliday ended the feud between themselves and the Clanton family with the bloody shoot-out at the OK Corral. Warren died before the battle, but the two other Earps and Holliday survived.

THE GUNFIGHTERS

EARTH
A small blue planet inhabited by humans. The Doctor has shown persistent interest in the affairs of Earth and his visits there are too numerous to record. During his third incarnation he was exiled there and prevented several invasion attempts. This fertile planet has attracted seemingly undue attention from marauding aliens including the Cybermen and the Daleks. Many of the Doctor's companions have been Earthlings and he confesses that they are one of his favourite species, capable of great evil and great good.

ECKERSLEY
A traitorous mining engineer from the planet Earth who, in league with the Ice Warriors, used deadly projections of the sacred beast Aggedor to halt work in the trisilicate mines of Peladon. He and Aggedor perished, killing each other.

THE MONSTER OF PELADON
See also *Aggedor, Ice Warriors, Peladon*

EDEN
A jungle planet, inhabited by man-eating plants and Mandrels, a segment of which was captured within the CET machine.

NIGHTMARE OF EDEN
See also *Mandrels*

EDGEWORTH, PROFESSOR
Edgeworth alias Azmael, an old Time Lord tutor and friend of the Doctor, was the benevolent ruler of the planet Joconda. When deposed by Mestor, Azmael employed desperate measures to defeat him. Drained in the mental dissolution of his opponent and devoid of further regenerations Asmail died in the arms of the Doctor.

THE TWIN DILEMMA
See also *Mestor, Joconda*

EL AKIR
A sadistic Saracen warlord and misogynist. He captured Barbara, intending to force her into his harem, but she was rescued by the intervention of Ian and Haroun. El Akir was killed by Haroun, in retribution for the Saracen's murder of Haroun's wife and son.

THE CRUSADE

ELDERS
One of two races, the other being the Savages, who lived on a planet visited by the first Doctor. The Elders, though outwardly intelligent and civilised, used a machine to transfer living energy from the Savages to themselves. They were finally persuaded to destroy the machine and

Steven was elected to remain on the planet as leader to unite the two factions.

THE SAVAGES
See also *Savages*

ELDRAD
A silicon-based creature who designed the Solar Barriers to protect his planet, Kastria, from the crippling cold. He plotted to usurp power and was sentenced to obliteration. In retaliation he destroyed the Barriers. Eldrad's hand survived obliteration, falling to Earth where millions of years later it regenerated itself with the aid of Sarah Jane whom it had possessed. Eldrad persuaded the Doctor to return him to Kastria, where he perished on the planet he had destroyed.

THE HAND OF FEAR
See also *Kastria*

ELDRED, PROFESSOR
The Earth-based owner of a space museum, and former rocket engineer, Eldred regretted the introduction of the T-Mat – the contemporary mode of space travel, and initially refused to help when the T-Mat was rendered non-operational by the Ice Warriors.

THE SEEDS OF DEATH
See also *Ice Warriors*

ELIXIR OF LIFE
An amazing healing fluid found on Karn and formed by the action of fire on surrounding rock. It is guarded by the Sisterhood of the Flame, who use it to

sustain their eternal life. The Time Lords also use it to aid difficult regenerations.

THE BRAIN OF MORBIUS
See also *Karn*

ENGLAND
The area of the planet Earth to which the TARDIS most frequently returns.

See also *Earth*

ENLIGHTENMENT
She, and her companion, Persuasion, were Urbankans on Monarch's ship, their mental identity being retained by microchips within an android body. Originally revealing themselves in their natural frog-like form, they soon reappeared wearing human bodies and clothing startlingly similar to sketches supplied by Tegan. Both Enlightenment and Persuasion perished in a fight against Adric and the Doctor.

FOUR TO DOOMSDAY
See also *Monarch, Urbankans*

ERATO
A peaceful Tythonian ambassador who offered the planet Chloris unlimited amounts of metal in exchange for chlorophyll. Lady Adrasta stole his communication device and imprisoned him in a deep pit where, due to his massive green bulk and inability to communicate, he was regarded as a dangerous monster. For fifteen years Erato languished in the

pit, accidentally crushing occasional visitors. He was eventually rescued by the Doctor.

THE CREATURE FROM THE PIT
See also *Adrasta*

ERGON
A menacing vulture-like creature created from anti-matter by Omega.

ARC OF INFINITY
See also *Omega*

E-SPACE
Exo-Space is a totally separate universe from normal space. It is a universe containing Alzarius, the Tharils and the planet of the Great Vampire. Usually it is impossible to travel from Normal to E-Space, but the Tardis accidentally passed through to it via a void created by the CVE.

See also *Alzarius, CVE, Great Vampire, Tharils*

ESTRAM, SIR GILES
A pseudonym adopted by the Master on 12th century Earth, where he attempted to pervert history by using Kamelion to impersonate King John.

THE KING'S DEMONS
See also *Kamelion*

ETERNALS
A race of immortals who indulged themselves by participating in a space race aboard replicas of ancient sea-going

vessels, complete with mortal crews from the appropriate periods.

ENLIGHTENMENT
See also *Wrack, Striker*

EXARIUS
The planet on which was to be found the Doomsday Weapon. It was the home of the Guardian, the Primitives and a colony of Earth people and was also desired for its minerals by the immoral IMC Company.

COLONY IN SPACE
See also *Guardian, IMC, Primitives*

EXXILON
A planet rich in parrinium, and abode of a once-brilliant race who created a living, thinking city which eventually exiled its inhabitants and began draining energy from the planet. The expelled Exxilons developed into two separate factions, one savage degenerates inhabiting the surface and worshipping the city, the others, including Bellal, friendly underground dwellers. The Doctor reluctantly destroyed the city, freeing the TARDIS and the planet from its destructive influence.

DEATH TO THE DALEKS
See also *Bellal*

EYE OF HARMONY
Rassilon, the first Time Lord, captured the nucleus of a Black Hole, stabilised it and housed it beneath the Panopticon. This is the Eye of Harmony which provided the energy source to power Gallifrey and made Time Travel available to its inhabitants. He also created the Great Key (the only means of access to the Eye) and the Sash, which protects the wearer from its powers.

See also *Gallifrey, Rassilon*

EYE OF HORUS
Designed by Horus and housed in the Pyramids of Mars, the Eye emitted radio signals which imprisoned Horus's evil brother, Sutekh, on Earth.

THE PYRAMIDS OF MARS
See also *Sutekh*

F

FANG ROCK

A misty rock supporting a lighthouse which was invaded by a Rutan in the early twentieth century. All the inhabitants perished.

HORROR OF FANG ROCK
See also *Rutans*

FARREL, REX

The weak young owner of a plastics factory who was hypnotised, used and eventually killed as a scapegoat for the Master.

THE TERROR OF THE AUTONS
See also *Autons*

FEDERATION, GALACTIC

An alliance of planets to which Peladon was eventually admitted. The other members included Earth, Mars, Arcturus and Alpha Centauri.

THE CURSE OF PELADON
THE MONSTER OF PELADON

FEDERICO, COUNT

The machinating uncle of Giuliano, the rightful ruler of San Martino. Federico plotted his nephew's death, but was himself killed by the Mandragora Helix.

THE MASQUE OF MANDRAGORA
See also *Giuliano*

FENDAHL

A gestalt creature consisting of a core and twelve Fendahleen, which resemble giant slugs. The Fendahl feeds and grows on death. It was believed to have perished in the destruction of the Fifth Planet, but a skull containing the Fendahl's dormant energy landed on Earth where it was discovered 12 million years later. Reactivated by the Time Scanner, it took over Thea Ransome as the core, and proceeded to create Fendahleen from hapless humans. The Doctor destroyed the Fendahleen through the use of salt and a bomb and disposed of the skull in a Super Nova.

IMAGE OF THE FENDAHL

FENDELMAN, PROFESSOR

A scientist infected by the influence of the Fendahl over his ancestors. He innocently invented the Time Scanner which reanimated the Fendahl, and was shot by one of its followers.

IMAGE OF THE FENDAHL
See also *Fendahl*

FFINCH, LIEUTENANT ALGERNON

An English officer pursuing the Scottish at Culloden. He captured the Doctor, Ben and Jamie, but was subsequently captured by Polly who persuaded him to give them a safe conduct back to the TARDIS.

THE HIGHLANDERS

FIBULI, MISTER

A timid subordinate of the Pirate Captain

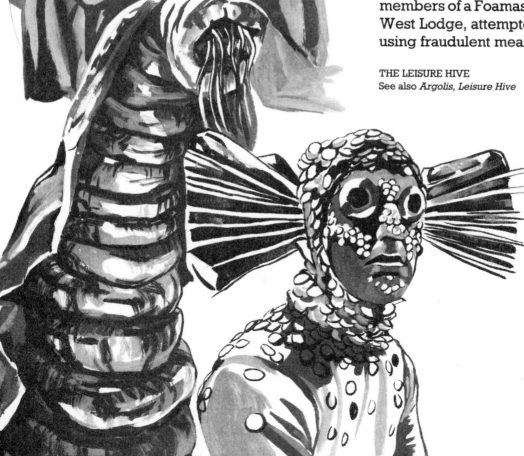

whose death in an explosion reduced the Captain to tears.

THE PIRATE PLANET

FISH PEOPLE
Certain human victims selected by the Atlanteans underwent an operation, which Polly narrowly avoided, enabling them to exist underwater. These slaveworkers provided food and were persuaded by the Doctor to take strike action to defeat Zaroff.

THE UNDERWATER MENACE
See also *Atlantis*

FOAMASI
Reptilian creatures who waged a twenty-minute war with the Argolin and left their enemies' planet a radiation-soaked wasteland. Immune to the radiation, members of a Foamasi political group, the West Lodge, attempted to buy Argolis using fraudulent means.

THE LEISURE HIVE
See also *Argolis, Leisure Hive*

FORESTER
A murderous Earthman who developed the toxic insecticide DN6. Despite having been miniaturised, the Doctor managed to alert the police, who arrested Forester.

PLANET OF GIANTS
See also *DN6*

FRANCE
A country visited by the Doctor during the French Revolution, the St Bartholomew's Day Massacre and the time disturbances created by Scaroth.

THE MASSACRE
CITY OF DEATH

FRONTIOS
A barren planet in the system of Veruna to which the remnants of mankind fled, escaping the disintegration of the Earth. Their spacecraft crashed mysteriously on the planet's surface sustaining irreparable damage and loss of life – the first in a series of unaccountable catastrophes which ultimately threatened the forty year old colony with extinction. Beneath Frontios' problems lay the Gravis but unofficial aid from the Doctor enhanced the survival prospects of earth's last outpost.

FRONTIOS
See also *Gravis, Plantagenet, Tractators*

GALAXY FIVE
The Galactic Federation needed Peladon's trisilicate to defeat Galaxy Five, with whom it was at war.

THE MONSTER OF PELADON
See also *Federation, Galactic*

GALAXY FOUR
The Rills escaped from a planet in this galaxy just before it exploded. The Drahvins were not so fortunate.

GALAXY FOUR
See also *Drahvins, Rills*

GALLEIA
The seductive queen of Atlantis at the time of the third Doctor's visit. She betrayed her husband, King Dalios, for the machiavellian charms of the Master. She died in the floods, realising her error too late.

THE TIME MONSTER
See also *Atlantis*

GALLIFREY
In the constellation of Kasteroborous lies Gallifrey, the planet of the Time Lords. Its inhabitants, not all of whom are Time Lords, live in domed cities, the largest being the Capitol – the centre of Time Lord life and ritual. In the wilderness beyond the domes live several tribes of outsiders or Shobogans.

The planet is powered by the Eye of Harmony captured by Rassilon, who also constructed the Transduction Barrier which renders Gallifrey virtually impregnable. Although aliens are forbidden, both Leela and Nyssa have visited Gallifrey – the former remaining there with Andred and K9. This is, perhaps, a measure of the Doctor's present standing with the Time Lords.

A dark area of Gallifrey, both physically and metaphorically, was the Death Zone, into which unfortunate aliens were lured to fight to the death for the entertainment of unscrupulous Time Lords. This sinister game was resurrected by Borusa, featuring the first five Doctors and many of their friends and enemies.

THE WAR GAMES – THE FIVE DOCTORS

GARM
A massive dog-faced creature, immune to radiation, who performed the dubious cure for Lazars' disease within the forbidden zone on Terminus. In return for saving the ship the Doctor destroyed the subsonic generator which supressed his free will.

TERMINUS

GARRON
An incorrigible conman who, with his sidekick Unstoffe, attempted to swindle the Graff Vynda Ka into buying Ribos.

THE RIBOS OPERATION
See also *Jethryk, Ribos*

GATHERER HADE
The Company tax-gatherer of the

Megropolis on Pluto. He was killed by the revolutionaries who overthrew the corrupt system.

THE SUNMAKERS

34

GAZTAKS
A band of space marauders whose leader, General Grugger, allied himself with Meglos. They all perished together on Zolfa-Thura.

MEGLOS

GEBEK
The leader of the Miners' Guild on Peladon who sought to reconcile his workers with Queen Thalira. He helped to defeat Eckersley and was made Chancellor.

THE MONSTER OF PELADON
See also *Eckersley, Peladon, Thalira*

GELL GUARDS
Omega's anti-matter servants. These shapeless blobs invaded UNIT HQ in search of the Doctor, ultimately transporting the whole building to Omega's anti-matter world.

THE THREE DOCTORS
See also *Omega*

GIULIANO
The handsome young heir to the dukedom of San Martino. He tried to persuade Sarah to remain with him in Renaissance Italy following the defeat of the Mandragora Helix.

THE MASQUE OF MANDRAGORA

GLOBAL CHEMICALS
An irresponsible corporation controlled by a megalomaniac computer, BOSS. Its dumping of chemical waste induced the Green Death.

THE GREEN DEATH
See also *BOSS, Green Death*

GONDS
The Kroton Machine stimulated and measured the intellect of the peaceful Gonds, selecting the most advanced to enter the machine. There they were drained of intelligence to awaken the sleeping Krotons. The Doctor released them from this malign influence.

THE KROTONS
See also *Dynatrope, Krotons*

GOTH, CHANCELLOR
A chancellor of the Time Lords who was corrupted into assassinating the president by the Master, and forced to duel with the Doctor in the Matrix. The ensuing mental strain killed him.

THE DEADLY ASSASSIN

GRAVIS
The Gravis, a Tractator wielding destructive gravitational powers and equally gruesome policies, manipulated its fellows on Frontios. By excavating a ring of tunnels beneath the planet it constructed a gravity motor to propel Frontios, the labour for which was provided by captive colonists, both living and dead. Using the TARDIS as bait, the Doctor immobilised the greedy Gravis and isolated it from its fellow Tractators, marooning it on the uninhabited planet of Kolkokron.

FRONTIOS
See also *Tractators, Frontios*

GRAFF VYNDA KA
A vicious warrior prince intent on regaining his lost Levithian empire. He died, raving mad, in an explosion on Ribos.

THE RIBOS OPERATION
See also *Ribos*

GRAVITRON
The Gravitron was a machine located on the Moonbase which regulated Earth's weather. The Cybermen attempted to destroy Earth with it, but were themselves the ultimate victims.

MOONBASE
See also *Cybermen*

GREAT CRYSTAL
A perfect crystal created by the molecular engineers on Manussa. Its ability to amplify thought and transform it into energy accidentally created the Mara. Defeated and banished to the dark places of the inside, they sought the crystal to regain their physical identity.

SNAKEDANCE
See also *Mara*

GREAT INTELLIGENCE
Exiled from another dimension, this malign disembodied entity used its power over human minds and the Yeti in its attempts to engulf Earth. The second Doctor defeated it on two occasions, only failing to destroy it completely by the misguided intervention of Jamie.

THE ABOMINABLE SNOWMAN
THE WEB OF FEAR
See also *Yeti*

GREAT KEY
The power of the Great Key, in conjunction with the other symbols of presidential office, was too dangerous to be possessed by one man. For generations the chancellor had sole knowledge of its whereabouts. The Doctor became the first president since Rassilon to handle the key which he used to activate the De-Mat Gun, thus foiling the Sontaran invasion of Gallifrey.

THE DEADLY ASSASSIN
THE INVASION OF TIME
See also *Rassilon*

GREAT ONE
The gigantic spider who ruled Metebelis Three. Crouched at the centre of a web of crystal, she needed the Doctor's crystal to complete the web which had enlarged her mind and body and commanded him to return it. The completed circuit destroyed her, and the radiation from her cave forced the Doctor to regenerate into his fourth body.

PLANET OF THE SPIDERS

GREAT VAMPIRE
The last and most malevolent of a ghoulish blood-sucking race, who were exterminated by the Time Lords. The Record of Rassilon states that one survived. The Doctor encountered him in E-Space, guarded by his servants Aukon, Zargo and Camilla. As the monster rose from its thousand-year sleep its heart was pierced by a rocket, programmed by the Doctor.

STATE OF DECAY
See also *Aukon, Camilla, Hydrax, Zargo*

GREEL, MAGNUS

See *Weng-Chiang*

GREEN DEATH
A deadly green slime, an effluent from Global Chemicals which contaminated and killed. It also produced a breed of murderous maggots.

THE GREEN DEATH
See also *BOSS*

GRENDEL
The scheming Count Grendal of Gracht plotted to usurp Prince Reynart's throne on Tara with replica androids. He escaped after a sword fight with the Doctor.

THE ANDROIDS OF TARA
See also *Tara*

GROVER, SIR CHARLES
This ruthless politician was transported back to Earth's prehistory by his own Operation Golden Age.

INVASION OF THE DINOSAURS
See also *Operation Golden Age*

GRUGGER, GENERAL

MEGLOS
See *Gaztaks*

GUARDIAN
A withered doll-like entity who lived in fire and guarded the Doomsday Machine which had devastated his race. He was persuaded by the Doctor to destroy the machine whose radiation had kept him alive.

COLONY IN SPACE
See also *Doomsday Weapon, Exarius, Primitives*

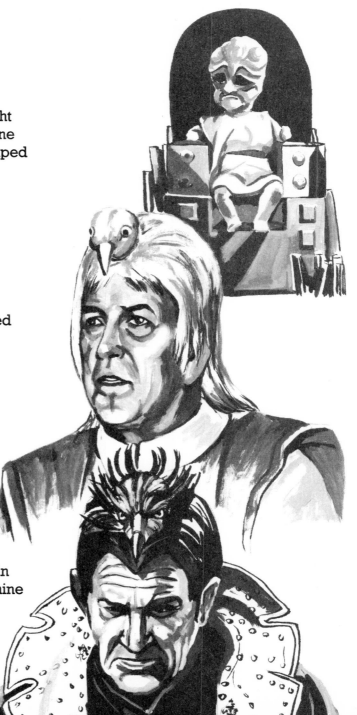

GUARDIAN, BLACK

Two equal and opposite forces balance the universe, one a power of order, the other of havoc. The Black Guardian desired the Key to Time as an instrument of chaos, vowing revenge on the Doctor who had destroyed it. To these ends he recruited Turlough. In a final confrontation between the two Guardians Turlough rejected evil, causing the Black Guardian to dissolve into flames.

THE RIBOS OPERATION – ENLIGHTENMENT
See also *Guardian, White, Turlough*

GUARDIAN, WHITE

The antithesis of the Black Guardian. He ordered the Doctor to recover the Key to Time to correct an imbalance in the universe.

THE RIBOS OPERATION – ENLIGHTENMENT
See also *Guardian, Black*

GULLIVER

A fictional character, created by Jonathan Swift, whom the Doctor encountered in the domain of the Mind Master, the Land of Fiction.

THE MIND ROBBER

GUNDAN

Axe-wielding robot warriors, built by slaves and programmed to kill the Tharils, who were, at one time, masters of an oppressive empire.

WARRIORS' GATE
See also *Tharils*

HAMPDEN, JANE

A Teacher in the village of Little Hodcombe. She and Tegan's grandfather, Andrew Verney, provided the sole opposition within the community to the fanatical war games.

THE AWAKENING
See also *Malus*

HARDIN

A tachyonics expert from Earth. He was a close friend of Mena whose life depended on his rejuvenation experiments with the tachyon generator.

THE LEISURE HIVE
See also *Argolis, Mena*

HARRY SULLIVAN

Lieutenant Harry Sullivan, a dashing young naval surgeon seconded to UNIT, became a somewhat confused companion of the fourth Doctor, whom he was assigned to look after following the latter's third regeneration. Lured aboard the TARDIS by the Doctor and Sarah, he proved a brave, if somewhat accident-prone, comrade. Having encountered several unsavoury species including Daleks and Cybermen, the TARDIS landed in contemporary Scotland where Harry declined the offer of a trip to London by TARDIS in favour of British Rail.

ROBOT – THE ANDROID INVASION

HAWTHORNE, MISS
The ebullient white witch of Devil's End who warned against the opening of the barrow which resurrected Azal's powers. Revelling in the ensuing fight against evil she refused to accept the Doctor's scientific explanations for events, firmly believing them to be the result of magic.

THE DAEMONS
See also *Azal, Bok*

HAYTER, PROFESSOR
A cynical passenger aboard the first Concorde kidnapped by the Master. A specialist on hypnosis, he resisted the hallucinations of normality which infected his fellow travellers, being convinced that their inhospitable environment was twentieth century Siberia. Hayter became absorbed by the life-force of the Xeraphin, thus enabling him to help Captain Stapely pilot the TARDIS.

TIME-FLIGHT
See also *Concorde, Xeraphin*

HEAT BARRIER
A massive force-field created by Azal around the village at Devil's End.

THE DAEMONS
See also *Azal*

HEDIN
A misguided Time Lord who attempted to assist Omega's return to Gallifrey. He atoned by saving the Doctor's life at the cost of his own. Unable to see the Doctor killed for his own crime, Hedin threw himself between the Doctor and the Castellan's gun.

ARC OF INFINITY
See also *Omega*

HENSELL
The governor of colony Vulcan. He was deceived by Lesterson as to the true nature of the Daleks and was ultimately exterminated by them.

THE POWER OF THE DALEKS

HEPESH
The high priest of Peladon during the Doctor's first visit, whose fears for his

planet's autonomy as a member of the Federation led him to plot against the ambassadors. He perished at the paws of Aggedor whom he had misused in his schemes.

THE CURSE OF PELADON
See also *Aggedor, Peladon*

HERRICK
An aggressive crew member of the Minyan spaceship searching for the P7E.

UNDERWORLD
See also *Minyos, Oracle*

HIERONYMOUS
This evil court astrologer was leader of the cult of Demnos in San Martino. He was the eager recipient of the Mandragora Helix energy, but when this was drained from him by the Doctor, nothing of Hieronymous remained.

THE MASQUE OF MANDRAGORA
See also *Demnos*

HIGH COUNCIL
The High Council of the Time Lords is the ultimate decision-making body on Gallifrey, consisting of the President, Chancellor, Castellan, a cardinal and a councillor.

See also *Time Lords*

HINDLE
A member of the Earth team inhabiting the Dome on Deva Loka, Hindle became increasingly unbalanced as the influence of the Mara asserted itself, intent upon pursuing a policy of 'Fire and Acid Purification' around the area of the Dome. He was distracted by the Box of Jana, through which he regained his sanity.

KINDA
See also *Mara*

HOBSON
The director of the Moonbase housing the Gravitron which was invaded by the Cybermen in the year 2070.

THE MOONBASE
See also *Gravitron*

HOLLIDAY
A notorious gunfighter and drunk who participated in the shoot-out at the OK Corral. After having a tooth extracted by Holliday the Doctor was mistaken for him by the Clanton gang.

THE GUNFIGHTERS

HORDA
These ravenous, white, snake-like creatures inhabited a pit which was used by the Sevateen as a trial by ordeal.

THE FACE OF EVIL
See also *Sevateen*

HORUS
The leader of the Osirians who, with his fellows, hunted down his evil brother Sutekh and imprisoned him on Earth.

PYRAMIDS OF MARS
See also *Eye of Horus, Sutekh*

HUGO
Hugo was an interplanetary policeman despatched to recover the twins, Romulus and Remus, abducted by Professor Edgeworth. Having been rescued by the Doctor from the remains of his crashed ship, extricated his boot from a Gastropod's gummy trail and rescued the twins, Hugo elected to remain on Joconda to establish order in the wake of Edgeworth's death.

THE TWIN DILEMMA
See also *Edgeworth, Mestor*

HUTCHINSON, SIR GEORGE
The psychic medium possessed by the Malus. Through him the antagonistic energy of the war games was absorbed by the awakening alien. Sir George was precipitated into the creature's lair, destroying them both.

THE AWAKENING
See also *Malus*

HYDRAX
The Dark Tower, menacing abode of 'The Three who Rule', was originally an Earth spaceship, the *Hydrax*. The Doctor detached one of its turrets, a space shuttle, to destroy the monster.

STATE OF DECAY
See also *Aukon, Camilla, Great Vampire, Zargo*

HYDROMEL
A precious drug taken by the Vanir to counteract the effects of radiation from the forbidden zone on Terminus. Nyssa remained behind to synthesise adequate amounts of hydromel, previously savagely rationed by the company controlling Terminus.

TERMINUS
See also *Terminus*

HYMETUSITE
The most radioactive substance in the galaxy which was brought to Skonnos as a tribute to the Nimon and used to fuel their space capsules.

THE HORNS OF NIMON
See also *Nimon*

I

IAN CHESTERTON

A science teacher at Coal Hill School, England. He and his colleague, Barbara Wright, became the first Doctor's unwilling companions when they forced entry to the TARDIS in search of a disturbingly knowledgable pupil, Susan. After many journeys, during which Ian was knighted by Richard the Lionheart, he and Barbara returned to twentieth century England in a Dalek time machine.

AN UNEARTHLY CHILD – THE CHASE

ICE WARRIORS

This powerful reptilian race of militaristic Martians, imposing in their Viking-like helmets and scaly green armour, are usually commanded by a warlord, physically more streamlined, intelligent and aristocratic, but equally as ruthless. The Doctor first encountered them frozen beneath the ice during Earth's second Ice Age. He also discovered their major weakness – vulnerability to heat. Having thwarted their two attempted invasions of Earth the Doctor entered into an uneasy alliance with them to ensure Peladon's admittance to the Federation. A return visit revealed more sinister motives towards Peladon, which they invaded, posing as a peace-keeping force, to steal the planet's deposits of trisilicate.

THE ICE WARRIORS – THE MONSTER OF PELADON
See also *Izlyr, Mars, Peladon, Varga*

IMC

The Interplanetary Mining Corporation demanded unquestioning loyalty from employees such as Captain Dent, who used ruthless methods to denude planets of their mineral deposits. Their arrival on the planet Exarius precipitated a bloody battle between themselves and the colonists, the IMC survivors of which were returned to Earth to stand trial.

COLONY IN SPACE
See also *Dent, IMC Robot*

INFERNO

A drilling project developed by Professor Stahlman to extract a new energy source, Stahlman's Gas, from the Earth's crust. The drilling released a green fluid which seeped up the drill hole, mutating all who came into contact with it into Primords. Transported to a parallel Earth where Project Inferno was on the point of destroying the planet, the Doctor was confronted by ruthless, virtually identical counterparts of the Brigadier, Benton and Liz Shaw.

INFERNO
See also *Primords*

INTER MINOR

This xenophobic planet had recently opened its frontiers when Vorg and Shirna arrived with their scope, containing a selection of miniaturised aliens including the Doctor and Jo.

CARNIVAL OF MONSTERS
See also *Scope*

INTERNATIONAL ELECTROMATIX

An electronics and computer company with a virtual worldwide monopoly whose managing director, the devious Tobias Vaughn, was in league with the Cybermen. Their attempted invasion of Earth was triggered by a radio signal which activated all IE Equipment, producing a hypnotic effect of global proportions.

THE INVASION
See also *Vaughn*

IONISER

The ioniser was developed to contain Earth's second Ice Age by intensifying the Sun's heat on small areas of the planet. It was also used to destroy the spacecraft of the Ice Warriors which was embedded in the ice.

THE ICE WARRIORS
See also *Ice Warriors, Varga*

IRONGRON

A shabby medieval robber chief, he tolerated the Sontaran Linx's presence in his seedy castle in return for promises of fabulous weapons. Discovering that the departure of Linx's spaceship would devastate his castle, Irongron attacked him and was gunned down by the Sontaran.

THE TIME WARRIOR
See also *Lynx, Sontarans*

ISSIGRI

Jointly owned by Dom Issigri and Milo Clancey, this mining company was one of

the first to exploit the precious mineral argonite. Following the mysterious disappearance of Dom Issigri, his daughter Madelaine took over, persuaded by the space pirate Caven who held Dom hostage.

THE SPACE PIRATES
See also *Argonite, Clancey*

IVO
A member of the rebels on the Great Vampire's planet. Following the murder of his son he led an attack on the tower. He eventually became joint leader of the village with Kalmar.

STATE OF DECAY
See also *Great Vampire*

IZLYR
An Ice Warrior Warlord and ambassador to Peladon, he helped the Doctor uncover the conspiracy to prevent Peladon's entry into the Federation.

THE CURSE OF PELADON
See also *Federation, Ice Warriors, Peladon*

J

JACKSON
The weary, but determined, commander of the Minyan space crew whose 100,000 year quest to recover the missing race bank of his people finally came to fruition aboard the P7E.

UNDERWORLD
See also *Oracle*

JAGAROTH
These one-eyed, green-skinned monstrosities ranked among the most vicious conquering races in the Universe. Fleeing from their devastated planet they landed on a totally barren alien world, Earth. Whilst attempting lift-off from this inhospitable planet their spaceship exploded, creating the conditions from which life began on Earth, but at the same time killing all the Jagaroth but one – Scaroth.

CITY OF DEATH
See also *Scaroth*

JAGO, HENRY GORDON
The owner of the Palace Theatre in Victorian London, beneath which lurked Magnus Greel, alias Weng-Chiang. Although a somewhat apprehensive sleuth, Jago helped Professor Litefoot and the Doctor who, he assumed, was from Scotland Yard, to track Weng-Chiang to his lair and destroy him.

THE TALONS OF WENG CHIANG
See also *Weng-Chiang*

JAMIE McCRIMMON

James Robert McCrimmon, a piper with the Young Pretender's army at Culloden, encountered the Doctor whilst escaping from the massacre with his clan chief, Colin McLaren. Taken aboard the TARDIS for his own safety he travelled with the Doctor throughout virtually the whole of his second incarnation, his fierce courage, cunning and total loyalty more than compensating for his lack of intelligence. When Victoria joined the TARDIS crew Jamie became strongly attached to her and was inconsolable when she left, although the arrival of Zoe soon remedied this situation. Following their adventures in the War Zones the Doctor, Zoe and Jamie were captured by the Time Lords who returned Jamie to Scotland in 1746, with all memory of the Doctor, save for their first adventure, erased.

THE HIGHLANDERS – THE TWO DOCTORS

JANIS THORN

Leela's constant, callous use of this deadly weapon, grown on her home planet, deeply angered the Doctor. When driven beneath the skin the poisonous thorn induced instant paralysis followed by death.

THE FACE OF EVIL
See also *Leela*

JANO

Jano, the leader of the Elders, used his Entity Transference Machine upon the first Doctor, thus imbuing himself with much of the Doctor's personality and morality. Emerging a changed, more enlightened man, he persuaded his people to destroy the machine.

THE SAVAGES
See also *Elders, Savages*

JETHRYK

This extremely scarce and precious mineral, transported to Ribos by the devious Garron, proved to be the first segment of the Key to Time.

THE RIBOS OPERATION
See also *Garron, Key to Time*

JOCONDA
Under the rule of Professor Edgeworth, Joconda was reputably a beautiful planet. Mestor's reign, however, substituted the slug-induced desolation which featured in Jocondan mythology.

THE TWIN DILEMMA
See also *Edgeworth, Hugo, Mestor*

JO GRANT
Cheeky, scatterbrained Jo Grant infiltrated UNIT by virtue of her influential uncle in the United Nations, and was introduced to the third Doctor as his new assistant by an amused Brigadier Lethbridge-Stewart. Eager to prove her worth, accident-prone Jo immediately launched herself into the Doctor's work, ruining one of his experiments and narrowly avoiding blowing him up. Their relationship, however, flourished. Although frequently terrified by alien menaces, in particular the Master, Jo remained stoically loyal to the Doctor. When she left him to marry Professor Jones, the Time Lord was visibly shattered.

TERROR OF THE AUTONS – THE GREEN DEATH
See also *Jones, Professor*

JONES, PROFESSOR
Professor Cliff Jones, a scientist and Nobel Prize winner for his ecology work on DNA synthesis, had established the Wholeweal community in Llanfairfach, Wales, which researched into alternative foods and energy sources. He and the Doctor defeated the menace of the Giant Maggots and, during the process, Jo fell in love with and agreed to marry the dedicated young scientist who was, in so many ways, reminiscent of the Doctor.

THE GREEN DEATH
See also *Jo Grant, Global Chemicals*

K

K9
There were three versions of this canine robot, the original of which was given to the Doctor by its creator, Professor Marius. A mobile computer in the form of a dog complete with wagging tail, antenna, stun gun and numerous other devices, K9 proved invaluable to the Doctor who became quite affectionate towards the little automaton.

When K9 elected to leave his master, remaining with Leela on Gallifrey, the Doctor built K9 Mark Two, a new, improved, accident-prone version. Having recently recovered from decapitation at the hands of the Marshmen, K9's vital circuits were damaged by the Time Winds, forcing him to remain in E-Space with Romana. K9 Mark Three was a present from the Doctor to his former companion Sarah-Jane Smith. He futilely attempted to forewarn his mistress of the onrushing malign force which transported her to the Death Zone on Gallifrey.

THE INVISIBLE ENEMY – THE FIVE DOCTORS; also 'K9 and Company'
See also *Marius*

KAFTAN
She and her colleague Klieg were ruthless logicians bent on releasing the Cybermen from their tombs on Telos. The success of the mission resulted in her death at the hands of the Cybermen.

THE TOMB OF THE CYBERMEN
See also *Cybermen, Klieg, Telos*

KAL

This savage caveman attempted to depose Za, the leader of the Tribe of Gum, by forcing the captive Doctor to produce fire. A gruesome fight to the death ensued between the two cavemen of which Kal was the loser.

THE TRIBE OF GUM
See also *Za*

KALEDS

The militaristic natives of the planet Skaro faced gradual extermination due to the effects of the continuous war of attrition between themselves and their hated fellow inhabitants, the Thals. Davros, their brilliant scientist, created a protective dome around the city and strove, via genetic mutation, to produce the ultimate specimen of the Kaled race, capable of surviving on their radiation-soaked planet. The crippled war victims, the Mutos, were expelled from the city to roam the wastelands. Davros's ultimate creations were the Daleks. Facing opposition from his fellow Kaleds, Davros helped the Thals to almost totally annihilate his own race. The Daleks completed the job.

GENESIS OF THE DALEKS
See also *Daleks, Davros, Mutos*

KALID

A pseudonym of the Master who adopted the guise of an oriental magician whilst luring Concordes to Earth's past.

TIME FLIGHT

KALIK

Brother of Zarb, the president of Inter Minor, whose downfall he plotted by releasing a Drashig from the scope. The Drashig promptly ate him.

CARNIVAL OF MONSTERS
See also *Drashigs, Scope*

KAMELION

This android discovered by the Master on Xeriphas could assume the voice and form of any living being. Kamelion's unassertive personality became a battleground between the Master and Doctor under

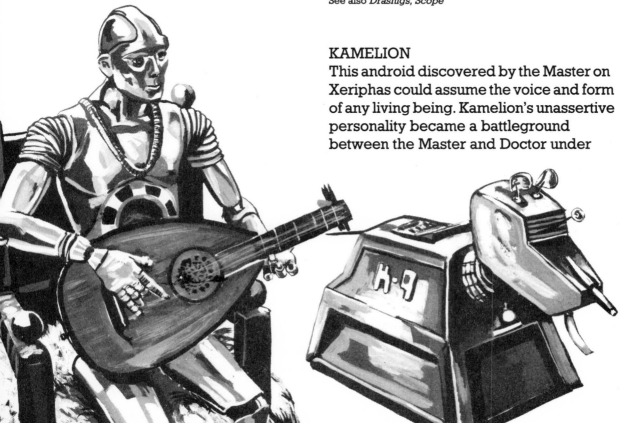

whose respective influences he assumed the likeness of King John, the Master, Doctor and Tegan. The Master, subjugating Kamelion yet again, lured the TARDIS to Sarn, where the distraught android, fearing further misuse, begged the Doctor to destroy him.

THE KING'S DEMONS
PLANET OF FIRE
See also *Xeriphas*

KALMAR
All knowledge was forbidden on the Great Vampire's planet, but the rebel scientist, Kalmar, endeavoured to rediscover technology. He eventually became joint leader with Ivo.

STATE OF DECAY
See also *Great Vampire, Ivo*

K'ANPO
A Time Lord and former guru of the Doctor, K'anpo had retired, living as a monk on Earth where he assisted with the Doctor's third regeneration. Following the assault of the Giant Spiders K'anpo regenerated into the waiting body of Cho-Je.

PLANET OF THE SPIDERS
See also *Spiders*

KARI
A brusque, accomplished space raider, she and Olvir landed on Terminus where they were abandoned by their superiors. Reluctantly at first, she helped the Doctor to unravel the deadly secret of Terminus.

TERMINUS
See also *Olvir, Terminus*

KARN
This desolate planet, in the same galaxy as Gallifrey, was laid waste by the wars of Morbius, who was eventually captured there and executed. The TARDIS, like many ships before it, was drawn to Karn by the psychic energy of the Sisterhood, the sole inhabitants apart from Solon, Condo and (unknown to them) Morbius.

THE BRAIN OF MORBIUS
See also *Morbius, Sisterhood of the Flame*

KASSIA
The wife of Tremas and stepmother of Nyssa, she tended the grove of the Melkur on Traken and fell under its evil influence. Fearing her husband's promotion to Keeper of Traken, a post which would take him from her, she co-operated with, and was killed by, the Master.

THE KEEPER OF TRAKEN
See also *Melkur, Nyssa, Tremas*

KASTRIA
An inhospitable planet whose only protection from the solar winds, the Solar Barriers, were created and later destroyed by Eldrad. Fearing his eventual return the silicon-based Kastrians committed voluntary genocide by destroying their race banks.

THE HAND OF FEAR
See also *Eldrad*

KATARINA
The handmaiden of Cassandra, she helped the wounded Steven to the TARDIS following the fall of Troy and was aboard it when it dematerialised. Katarina's time

with the Doctor was painfully brief as she sacrificed herself to save his life from the Daleks. The Doctor affectionately remembered her as a daughter of the gods.

THE MYTH MAKERS
THE DALEK MASTER PLAN

KELLER MACHINE
This machine, capable of cleansing minds of evil, housed within it a mind parasite which, by amplifying its victims' deepest fears, killed them. Even the Doctor and the Master were susceptible to its powers which grew with the evil it absorbed. It was eventually destroyed by a missile.

THE MIND OF EVIL

KELLMAN
A ruthless Earth scientist and agent of Vorus, he guided the Cybermen to Nerva Beacon, contributing to the deaths of the Beacon's inhabitants. He perished in a rock fall in the underground tunnels of Voga.

REVENGE OF THE CYBERMEN
See also *Cybermen, Voga, Vorus*

KELNER
This obsequious Castellan rapidly transferred his loyalties from the Doctor to the Vardans, and finally assisted the Sontarans in their invasion of Gallifrey.

THE INVASION OF TIME
See also *Sontarans, Vardans*

KEMBEL
The planet from which the Daleks launched their Master Plan, killing Marc Cory and devastating Kembel with the Time Destructor.

MISSION TO THE UNKNOWN
THE DALEK MASTER PLAN

KENT, GILES
He persuaded the Doctor to help depose the evil Salamander, but was revealed to be as ruthless and ambitious as his leader. Salamander eventually shot him.

ENEMY OF THE WORLD
See also *Salamander*

KERENSKY, PROFESSOR
A naive, timid little scientist who, funded by Count Scarlioni, alias Scaroth, invented the field generator which was responsible for the Paris time slips. Forced within the range of his own machine he was aged to death by Scaroth.

CITY OF DEATH
See also *Jagaroth, Scaroth*

KETTLEWELL, PROFESSOR
Creator of the prototype robot K1, this misguided professor, seduced by dreams of a pollution-free world, aided Miss Winters in her plans for world domination. Eventually recognising his naivety, Kettlewell attempted to make amends. Throwing himself between Sarah, Harry and the robot he was disintegrated.

ROBOT
See also *Giant Robot, Winters*

KEYS OF MARINUS
The first Doctor and his companions searched for the five keys which operated

the Conscience of Marinus. One proved to be a fake, and, when introduced into the machine, destroyed it.

THE KEYS OF MARINUS
See also *Conscience, Voord*

KEY TO TIME
The six segments of this awesomely powerful cube, dispersed throughout Time and Space, were required by the White Guardian to restore the balance of the universe. The Doctor and Romana were dispatched to locate and recover them. The Black Guardian also desired the Key as an instrument of universal chaos and by confronting the Doctor in the guise of the White Guardian almost achieved his aim. Discovering the deception the Doctor re-scattered the segments.

The six segments of the Key were a lump of jethryk, the planet Calufrax, the Seal of Diplos, part of a Taran statue, a holy relic of the Swampies and Princess Astra.

THE RIBOS OPERATION – THE ARMAGEDDON FACTOR
See also *Black and White Guardians*

KINDA
A peaceful race of intelligent telepaths inhabiting Deva Loka, most of whom were mute. Only the wisest female, Panna, and her successor, Karuna, had the gift of speech until the Mara returned, infiltrating Aris. The Doctor freed the Kinda from the Mara's influence.

KINDA
See also *Panna*

KLIEG, ERIC
An insane logician who, with his colleague Kaftan resurrected the Cybermen of

Telos. They rewarded him with strangulation.

THE TOMB OF THE CYBERMEN
See also *Cybermen, Telos*

KOQUILION
Ostensibly a menacing, tusked creature protecting Vicki and Bennett from the Didonians. In reality he was Bennett, who had murdered his colleagues and believed that he had also murdered the entire Didonian race. He assumed the disguise as an alibi to be confirmed on his return to Earth by the innocent Vicki. Bennett, terrified by the sudden appearance of living Didonians, plunged from a cliff to his death.

THE RESCUE
See also *Vicki*

KRAALS
The stocky, green Kraals had virtually destroyed themselves and their planet Oseidon in a series of atomic wars. The survivors, led by chief scientist Styggron, planned to invade Earth with android replicas of humans, including versions of Sarah, Harry, Benton and the Doctor.

THE ANDROID INVASION
See also *Oseidon, Styggron*

KROLL
Initially a huge squid, when he swallowed the fifth segment of the Key to Time he assumed colossal proportions, over five miles long. Worshipped by the Swampies of Delta Three, Kroll was aroused from a deep hibernation by the drilling

operations of a methane refinery which he promptly attacked. The Doctor reconverted the segment, destroying Kroll.

THE POWER OF KROLL
See also *Key to Time*

KRONOS
The time monster, Kronos the Kronovore, was summoned to Earth by the Master's time machine, TOMTIT. Unable to control the powerful being, the Master travelled to Atlantis where, using the Crystal of Kronos, he commanded it to annihilate the mythical city. Released from the Master's power by the Doctor, Kronos granted the two Time Lords their freedom.

THE TIME MONSTER
See also *Atlantis*

KROTONS
Blind crystalline creatures of pure tellurium, who were reanimated by the intelligence of the Doctor and Zoe. The Krotons planned to relaunch their ship, the Dynatrope, an action which would destroy the Gonds, but the Doctor prevented this by dissolving their tellurium structure with acid.

THE KROTONS
See also *Dynatrope*

KRYNOID
Travelling in pairs from deep space, two seed pods of this intelligent parasite weed fell to Earth and were frozen in the permafrost. The first, eventually destroyed by the Doctor, burst, infecting

its human host and converting him into a Krynoid, a carnivorous plant which when fully grown spores, releasing thousands of lethal pods into the atmosphere. The second Krynoid, taller than a house and controlling the surrounding plant life, was destroyed by Phantom jets just prior to germination.

THE SEEDS OF DOOM
See also *Chase*

KUBLAI KHAN
The emperor of Mongol China to whom Marco Polo intended to present the TARDIS as a gift. During a game of backgammon between the Doctor and the amicable old Khan, the Doctor won fabulous prizes but gambled away the TARDIS.

MARCO POLO

KY
A Solonian war chief whose successful metamorphosis, from humanoid, through mutant, to his ultimate form, a beautiful golden being, was finally accomplished with the aid of the Doctor, the Solonian Crystal, and a heavy dose of Thaesium radiation.

THE MUTANTS
See also *Mutants, Solos*

Clockwise from top left: The Malus which infiltrated the TARDIS, Professor Marius, Maren the Malus in Little Hadcombe Church and Richard Mace.

Clockwise from top left: One of Sutekh's deadly Mummies, a Muto from Skaro, a Mutt from Solos and the Morbius Monster.

*From top: The Movellans, a Monoid,
Mena of the Leisure Hive and Morgus
of Androzani Major.*

Clockwise from top left: The Mandrels, a Melkur, a Marshman, Meglos in the guise of the fourth Doctor and a Mechonoid.

L

LATEP
One of a small group of Thals who travelled to the planet Spiridon to destroy a vast army of Daleks housed there. His mission completed, he asked Jo to remain with him, but she declined.

PLANET OF THE DALEKS

LAZAR'S DISEASE
The victims of this highly contagious, terminal disease were shipped to Terminus where the potential cure, exposure to large doses of radiation, often proved fatal. Nyssa, surviving both infection and remedy, remained on Terminus to perfect the hazardous cure.

TERMINUS
See also *Garm, Terminus, Vanir*

LAZLO
A Tharil slave aboard Rorvik's ship, he rescued Romana and passed through the Warriors' Gate with her and his people.

WARRIORS' GATE
See also *Rorvik, Tharils*

LEELA
The Tesh and the Sevateem, newly reconciled and embracing peace, nominated Leela, a warrior of the Sevateem, as their leader. Horrified at the prospect, she forced her entry into the TARDIS, preferring danger and adventure with the Doctor. His constant attempts to civilise this knife-wielding savage clad in animal skins were largely frustrated. Her 'if in doubt, kill it' mentality often drove him to distraction. Paradoxically it was Leela's instinct and prowess with virtually any weapon which often proved his salvation. Having helped to defeat the Sontaran invasion, Leela decided to remain on Gallifrey with Andred and K9.

THE FACE OF EVIL – THE INVASION OF TIME
See also *Sevateem, Tesh*

LEISURE HIVE

Built by the Argolin, it was a massive amusement complex promoting universal racial harmony. Housed within it were the Tachyon Generator and Experiential Grid, offering variable environments designed to stimulate physical, psychic and intellectual regeneration. Sabotaged by Brock, a Foamasi agent, the Hive became a potential death trap.

THE LEISURE HIVE
See also *Argolis, Tachyon Generator*

LESTER

One of the few survivors of the Cyberman invasion of Nerva Beacon. He, Stevenson and the Doctor, wearing explosive devices, were transported to Voga by the Cybermen where Lester sacrificed his life for the others, exploding his bomb in a fight with the Cybermen.

REVENGE OF THE CYBERMEN
See also *Voga*

LESTERSON

The chief scientist of Vulcan Colony, he foolishly reanimated a Dalek, believing it to be a potentially invaluable robot. His dawning realisation of the Dalek's true character, driven home by the sight of hundreds of fully armed Daleks pouring off a production line, unbalanced Lesterson who was subsequently exterminated.

THE POWER OF THE DALEKS

LEXA

The leader of the Deons guarding and worshipping the mythical powers of the Dodecahedron. Having previously sentenced the Doctor to death Lexa sacrificed her own life to save Romana from General Grugger.

MEGLOS
See also *Dodecahedron*

LI-H'SEN CHANG

A Chinese magician and music hall performer whose innocent act featuring Mister Sin belied his true purpose, that of procuring young female victims for his master Weng-Chiang. Chang believed Weng Chiang to be a Chinese god and, having displeased him, perished in the London sewers, the victim of a giant rat.

THE TALONS OF WENG-CHIANG
See also *Weng-Chiang*

LINX

Referred to as 'toad-face' by his reluctant host Irongron, Linx, a marooned Sontaran officer, constructed a primitive time machine transporting twentieth century scientists back to medieval England to repair his ship. As the ship took off Linx was killed by an arrow which penetrated his probic vent.

THE TIME WARRIOR
See also *Irongron, Sontarans*

LITEFOOT, PROFESSOR

An independently-minded Victorian scientist and pathologist, he possessed Weng-Chiang's time cabinet without being aware of its true function. Fascinated by a sudden spate of mysterious deaths, he and Jago helped the Doctor defeat Weng-Chiang.

THE TALONS OF WENG-CHIANG
See also *Jago*

LIZ 79

A decrepit old spacecraft belonging to Milo Clancey, in which he rescued the Doctor and his companions.

THE SPACE PIRATES
See also *Clancey*

LITTLE HODCOMBE

The venue for Sir George Hutchinson's 1984 war games, recreating in disturbing realism the events perpetrated there during the English Civil War of 1643.

THE AWAKENING
See also *Jane Hampden, Hutchinson, Malus*

LIZ SHAW

A highly intelligent Cambridge scientist who was recruited by the Brigadier, becoming UNIT's scientific expert. The arrival of the newly-generated third Doctor, however, virtually relegated her to the role of assistant. Having helped the Doctor to defeat several alien menaces she left UNIT to pursue her own career at Cambridge.

SPEARHEAD FROM SPACE – INFERNO

LOCATORMUTOR CORE

The fourth Doctor was entrusted with this instrument by the White Guardian. Its function was to locate and then transform the individual segments of the Key to Time back to their original form.

THE RIBOS OPERATION – THE ARMAGEDDON FACTOR
See also *Key to Time*

LOCH NESS MONSTER

Brought to Earth as an embryo by the Zygons, the monster, or Skarasen, produced lactic fluid on which the Zygons existed. Having been converted into a Cyborg, it homed in on Broton's signals, destroying oil rigs and eventually swimming up the Thames. Having swallowed the homing device it returned to its adopted home of Loch Ness.

TERROR OF THE ZYGONS
See also *Zygons*

LOGAR

A mythical silver clad spirit of the volcano, worshipped by the people of Sarn. The legend originated when Trion spacetravellers visited the planet.

PLANET OF FIRE
See also *Sarn*

LOGIN

A respected member of the Starliner who was chosen as a Decider, his predecessor having been killed by the Marshmen. He proved more capable of decision-making than his two colleagues and, under his guidance, the Starliner finally left Alzarius.

FULL CIRCLE
See also *Alzarius, Marshmen, Starliner*

LOGOPOLIS

A planet inhabited by monk-like logicians whose continuous calculations (Block Transfer Computations) had maintained the existence of the universe beyond its point of total collapse. The centrepoint of Logopolis was a mathematical reproduction of Earth's Pharos Project. Unaware of the significance of the planet, the Master unbalanced its complex structure, spreading entropy across the universe and ultimately destroying Logopolis.

LOGOPOLIS
See also *Block Transfer Computations, Pharos Project*

LON

An indolent young noble, son of the Federator on Manussa. He was used by the Mara to regain the Great Crystal.

SNAKEDANCE
See also *Great Crystal, Mara*

LUPTON

In his hunger for power, Lupton misused the rituals of the Meditation Centre, accidentally summoning the Giant Spiders of Metebelis Three to Earth in search of their missing crystal. Crouched invisibly on his back, her mind linked to his, a Spider granted Lupton amazing powers enabling him to teleport to Metebelis where, having deeply offended the Spiders, he was eaten.

PLANET OF THE SPIDERS
See also *Metebelis Crystal, Metebelis Three, Spiders*

LYTTON

Lytton, a ruthless commander of troopers employed by the Daleks, was despatched to release Davros from his icy imprisonment. He journeyed with the Daleks down a time corridor to twentieth century Earth, participating in the ensuing devastation. Ominously Lytton and two troopers survived the denouement, escaping through London's docklands disguised as police officers.

RESURRECTION OF THE DALEKS
ATTACK OF THE CYBERMEN

McLAREN, COLIN
Jamie's clan chief. He was wounded at Culloden, captured by the English (along with the Doctor, Ben and Jamie) and finally rescued by his daughter, Kirsty, and Polly. The Laird, his daughter and the liberated Scots sailed to safety in France.

THE HIGHLANDERS
See also *Jamie*

MACE, RICHARD
An itinerant thespian who, flourishing a brace of pistols, rescued the Doctor and his companions from a group of footpads in plague-ridden England. A reluctant hero, Mace contributed to the defeat of the Terileptils, then remained in London to combat the Great Fire of 1666, accidentally started by the Doctor.

THE VISITATION
See also *Terileptils*

MACRA
A race of giant crablike parasites who existed on toxic gas mined by a brainwashed colony of apparently contented humans. The Doctor disconnected their gas supply, thereby destroying them

THE MACRA TERROR

MAGGOTS
Breeding in the mines below Global Chemicals, mutated and nurtured by its effluent green slime, these ravenous monsters slowly burrowed to the surface, stalking Jo and infecting Cliff Jones with the Green Death. The Doctor, pursued by a mature maggot, by now a giant flying insect, destroyed the remainder with a fungicide solution, thereby preventing their mass metamorphosis.

THE GREEN DEATH
See also *Global Chemicals, Professor Jones*

MAGMA CREATURES
Reptilian carnivores who inhabited the lower levels of the caves of Androzani Minor.

THE CAVES OF ANDROZANI

MAILER, HARRY
A hardened inmate of Stangmoor Prison, Mailer avoided processing by the Keller Machine and instigated a riot, kidnapping the Doctor and Jo at gunpoint. The weapon was shot from his hand by the Brigadier.

THE MIND OF EVIL
See also *Keller Machine*

MAITLAND
The captain of a spaceship immobilised by the Sensorites. Upon his oath to reveal nothing of the Sense Sphere or the abundance of Molybdenum his ship was released.

THE SENSORITES
See also *Sensorites, Molybdenum*

MALKON

Turlough's younger brother Malkon survived a crashlanding on the planet Sarn which killed his father, a political prisoner from Trion. The local inhabitants, interpreting the convict brand upon his arm as a mark of Logar's favour, revered him and raised the boy in ignorance of his origins. Having challenged his mentor Timanov, Malkon and his brother returned to Trion, their exiles rescinded.

THE PLANET OF FIRE
See also *Sarn, Trion, Turlough*

MALUS

The Malus was the abandoned spearhead of a postponed alien invasion of Earth. It lay dormant within the fabric of an ancient church until a Civil War massacre in 1643 aroused the malign entity by providing an infusion of violent psychic energy. In 1984 Sir George Hutchinson reawakened it in recreating the events of 1643, but his death and the resultant severance of its psychic links destroyed the Malus and the church it haunted.

THE AWAKENING
See also *Hutchinson*

MANDRAGORA HELIX

A spiral of pure energy controlled by a malign intelligence which, unknown to the Doctor, penetrated the TARDIS, and accompanied the Time Lord to fifteenth-century Italy. Possessing the followers of Demnos, it attempted to engulf the Earth. The Doctor drained away the Helix energy, but warned that the Earth might

face renewed attacks from Mandragora towards the end of the twentieth century.

THE MASQUE OF MANDRAGORA
See also *Hieronymous*

MANDRELS

Ferocious green-eyed monsters of the planet Eden which, at death, decompose into the highly addictive drug, Vraxoin. Several Mandrels escaped from the CET machine causing havoc before their recapture.

NIGHTMARE OF EDEN
See also *CET Machine, Vraxoin*

MARA

The snakelike Mara, which fed on evil, was unintentionally brought into being via the Great Crystal of the Manussans, whose civilisation it conquered, establishing a tyrannical empire which was eventually

defeated by the Federation. Banished to the 'dark places of the inside', the Mara struggled, by use of Tegan and the Kinda, to re-establish its physical form. Failing on Deva Loka when the Doctor surrounded it with mirrors, the Mara, dominating Tegan's dreams, returned to Manussa where it was destroyed by the Doctor while in the process of regaining its physical entity via the Great Crystal.

KINDA
SNAKEDANCE
See also *Great Crystal, Manussa*

MARCO POLO
The Doctor and his companions travelled with Marco Polo's caravan to the court of Kublai Khan, to whom the intrepid Venetian explorer intended to present the TARDIS as a gift. Polo returned the key to the TARDIS in recognition of the Doctor's help in defeating Tegana.

MARCO POLO
See also *Tegana*

MAREN
The high priestess of the Sisterhood on Karn, Maren was suspended in perpetual old age by the Elixir of Life. Although initially suspicious of the Doctor, she ultimately sacrificed her life for him, and gave him her share of the Elixir. She was consumed by the Sacred Flame.

THE BRAIN OF MORBIUS
See also *Elixir of Life*

MARINUS
The TARDIS crew traversed the planet of Marinus in search of the keys to the Conscience, encountering sands of glass, seas of acid, the city of the Morphotons, and the Voord.

THE KEYS OF MARINUS
See also *Conscience, Morphoton, Voord*

MARIUS, PROFESSOR
Formerly of New Heidelberg University, Earth, Marius worked at the Bi-Al Foundation, specialising in extra-terrestrial pathological endomorphisms (alien diseases). Aided by his computer dog, K9, he fought the virus infecting the Doctor until both he and K9 were temporarily contaminated. The Nucleus defeated, Marius returned to Earth leaving K9, who was unable to go with him, in the care of the Doctor.

THE INVISIBLE ENEMY
See also *Bi-Al Foundation, K9, Nucleus*

MARS
A planet in Earth's solar system which was once the home planet of the Ice Warriors. It also housed the Eye of Horus.

See also *Eye of Horus, Ice Warriors*

MARSHAL
The unprincipled commander of the Skybase who took sadistic pleasure in murdering the Mutants of Solos. Blackmailing the Doctor to assist his chief scientist, he exploded rockets on the planet's surface, intending to render the atmosphere suitable for Earth colonisation

but unbreathable to the native Solonians. He was killed by Ky.

THE MUTANTS
See also *Ky, Skybase, Solos*

MARSHMEN

The Marshmen were mid-way on the evolutionary cycle between spiders and humanoids, the ancestors of the Alzarians aboard the Starliner. Rising at Mistfall from the Alzarian swamps, the rapidly adapting creatures headed for the Starliner, decapitating K9 on the way.

FULL CIRCLE
See also *Alzarius, Starliner*

MASTER

The Master is the Doctor's opposite, though their histories contain many similarities: both studied together at the Time Lord academy, grew disillusioned and became renegades, each stealing a TARDIS to roam the universe. The Master, whose intellect is equal to the Doctor's, used his talents to dominate and destroy, perfecting his hypnotic powers and machiavellian charm to subjugate lesser species. The two clashed frequently on Earth during the third Doctor's exile, the Master instigating and assisting numerous alien invasions. Each Time Lord derived a perverse enjoyment from these encounters, perhaps because they were so equally matched, but the Doctor's consistent compassion towards his adversary was unreciprocated. Following the Master's machinations involving Earth, Draconia and the Daleks, he temporarily vanished from the Doctor's life, reappearing several years later to lure the fourth Doctor to their home planet, Gallifrey. Gone was the suave, elegant Master. Having reached the end of his cycle of regenerations he had become a hideously deformed and cowled skeleton, obsessed by hate and revenge, who struggled insanely to sustain his depleted life cycle, almost destroying Gallifrey in the attempt.

Grimly clinging to life, he became stranded on Traken as a Melkur, gathering power until, using the power of the Source of Traken, he was able to escape, stealing the body of Tremas. In this new body, physically reminiscent of that encountered by the third Doctor, the

Master, having precipitated the Doctor's fourth regeneration, resumed their feud and adopted various disguises to conceal his identity. Although the Master was somewhat unusually despatched by the Time Lords to aid the five Doctors in the Death Zone, he predictably used the situation to his own advantage, seeking the power of Rassilon and immortality. He remains one of the Doctor's most persistent and dedicated enemies.

TERROR OF THE AUTONS – MARK OF THE RANI
See also *Doctor, Melkur*

MATRIX
The total knowledge accumulated by the Time Lords is stored within the APC Net, made accessible to the President by one of the symbolic ornaments of Gallifrey, the Matrix crown. Linking with the Matrix can prove traumatic to an unprepared mind. The Doctor's fantasy duel with the Master within the APC Net almost killed him and his second link, on his presidential investiture, drove him into a coma.

THE DEADLY ASSASSIN
INVASION OF TIME
See also *APC Net*

MATTER CONDENSATION
A particularly gruesome mode of death employed by the Master, by which the body particles are shrunk, reducing the victim to a lifeless miniaturised doll.

See also *Master*

MAWDRYN
Mawdryn and his fellow scientists experimented with rejuvenation, but only succeeded in achieving the prospect of an eternity of bodily degeneration from which they sought release in death. To achieve this, the Doctor was almost compelled to sacrifice his remaining regenerations, but the confused intervention of two Brigadiers from separate time periods created a massive release of energy, saving the Doctor and granting death to Mawdryn and his companions.

MAWDRYN UNDEAD

MAXIMUS PETTULIAN
The first Doctor, mistaken for this murdered musician, was brought before Nero to play for him and became embroiled in the court intrigues of decadent Imperial Rome.

THE ROMANS

MAXTIBLE, THEODORE
The joint creator of a time machine with Edward Waterfield, this Victorian scientist was instrumental in the kidnap of his colleague's daughter, Victoria. Lured by promises of a device for transmuting metal into gold, Maxtible aided the Daleks in their quest to distill the Human Factor from Jamie, but was himself imbued with the Dalek Factor. He perished in a fight with a giant Turk on Skaro.

EVIL OF THE DALEKS
See also *Waterfield*

MECHANUS
The inhospitable vegetation of this jungle planet attacked the Doctor and his

61

companions who landed there, pursued by Daleks. It was also the home of the Mechonoids.

THE CHASE

MECHONOIDS
These lumpy spherical robots, originally built by humans, inhabited a metal city on the planet Mechanus. All life forms they encountered, including the marooned astronaut Steven Taylor, were regarded purely as subjects to study. The arrival of the Daleks precipitated a ferocious battle in which the Mechonoids, their city and the Daleks perished.

THE CHASE
See also *Mechanus*

MEDDLING MONK
This renegade Time Lord amused himself by attempting to pervert the course of Earth history. He offered King Harold atomic bazookas in 1066, but was foiled by the Doctor who removed the dimensional control from his TARDIS, stranding him on Earth. Having eventually repaired his machine, the Monk followed the Doctor to Tigus and ancient Egypt, seeking revenge. He was again outwitted by the Doctor who stole the Monk's directional unit, thus rendering his TARDIS unprogrammable.

THE TIME MEDDLER
THE DALEK MASTER PLAN

MEGARA
These floating justice machines were imprisoned in their own spaceship for 4,000 years by Cessair of Diplos whom they had convicted. The Doctor released the obsessive Megara who immediately attempted to convict and execute him over a formality. Having carried out their sentence of perpetual imprisonment on Cessair, the Doctor speedily dispatched them to Diplos.

THE STONES OF BLOOD
See also *Cessair of Diplos*

MEGLOS
Meglos, the last of the Zolfa-Thurans, was a green cactus-like alien with the ability to possess and alter the appearance of a captured body. Aided by the Gaztaks he immobilised the Doctor, impersonated him and stole the Dodecahedron, returning with it to the shields of Zolfa-Thura, his own highly destructive invention. He perished on his home planet in an explosion engineered by the Doctor.

MEGLOS
See also *Dodecahedron, Gaztaks*

MELKUR
A name used to describe evil entities who immediately calcify in the atmosphere of goodness pervading Traken. The Master remained a Melkur for several years, eventually escaping to wreak havoc on the peaceful planet.

THE KEEPER OF TRAKEN
See also *Master, Traken*

MENA
The capable chairwoman of the Leisure Hive and ruler of Argolis, she replaced her predecessor who aged to death with

alarming speed. Faced with an identical fate, Mena was rejuvenated by the Tachyon Generator perfected by Romana and Hardin.

THE LEISURE HIVE
See also *Argolis, Tachyon Generator*

MENOPTERA
Resembling a cross between giant butterflies and bees, these sensitive creatures became slaves of the Zarbi when the Animus invaded Vortis. Barbara's destruction of the Animus enabled the Zarbi and Menoptera to resume their peaceful co-existence.

THE WEB PLANET
See also *Animus, Optera, Vortis, Zarbi*

MENTALIS
A giant computer built by Drax for the Zeons which masterminded the Zeons' war strategy against Atrios.

THE ARMAGEDDON FACTOR
See also *Drax, Zeos*

MENTIADS
The mysterious and misunderstood psychic element of society on Zanak. They experienced the death throes of planets sucked dry by the Captain and used their telepathic powers to oppose him.

THE PIRATE PLANET
See also *Zanak*

MESTOR
One of the giant gastropods, this giant mind-reading slug plotted the demise of the planet Joconda by exploding a neighbouring star. The intense heat generated by the explosion would incubate his parasitic eggs, spreading

them throughout the universe. Mestor was foiled by Edgeworth and the Doctor who distracted and dissolved him.

THE TWIN DILEMMA
See also *Edgeworth, Joconda*

METAL VIRUS

This substance, which rapidly corrodes living metal, was invented by Professor Kettlewell and used by the Doctor to destroy the Giant Robot.

ROBOT
See also *Giant Robot*

METEBELIS CRYSTAL

The crystal was appropriated by the Doctor on a visit to Metebelis Three. It possessed strange qualities, focussing the powers of concentration and clearing the mind. The Doctor gave the blue crystal to Jo Grant as a wedding present, but she was reluctantly compelled to return it due to the disruptive effects it caused in the Amazon. An evil influence was exerted by the Metebelis Spiders who travelled to Earth in search of the crystal which, when recovered and inserted into the web of the Great One, destroyed her.

THE GREEN DEATH
PLANET OF THE SPIDERS
See also *Great One, Metebelis Three, Spiders*

METEBELIS THREE

This blue planet was inhabited by ruthlessly intelligent Giant Spiders and their human slaves, survivors of a crashed spaceship from Earth. The Doctor's removal of a valuable crystal on a previous visit almost resulted in his death when he returned.

PLANET OF THE SPIDERS
See also *Great One, Metebelis Crystal, Spiders*

MIND MASTER

The Mind Master lured the Doctor and his companions to a terrifying Land of Fiction where they encountered as adversaries various characters of fantasy including Gulliver, Medusa and the Minotaur. The Mind Master, a harmless old Victorian comic book writer, was forced to bring to life fictional characters by a huge computer controlling his mind and which attempted to persuade the Doctor to take his place. Zoe smashed the computer and released him.

THE MIND ROBBER
See also *Gulliver, Minotaur*

MINOTAUR

This supposedly mythical beast was encountered by the Doctor in the Land of Fiction and also in Atlantis where it guarded the Crystal of Kronos.

THE MIND ROBBER
THE TIME MONSTER
See also *Kronos, Nimon*

MINYOS

The Time Lords had accelerated the development of the primitive Minyans, exerting a benevolent influence in their affairs against which the Minyans eventually revolted. They then proceeded to annihilate their own planet with atomic weapons. Deeply shocked at the outcome of their intervention, the Time Lords henceforth pursued a policy of non-intervention in alien civilisations. Anticipating the devastation, a patrol vessel had been dispatched to locate the Minyan race bank aboard the P7E which had disappeared on route to a small colony on Minyos Two. It was these Minyans, still doggedly pursuing their quest through countless regenerations, that the Doctor encountered 100,000 years later. With his aid they finally recovered the lost race bank.

UNDERWORLD
See also *Oracle, P7E*

MIRA
The planet of the invisible and warlike Visians, upon which the first Doctor's party were surrounded by Daleks.

THE DALEK MASTER PLAN
See also *Visians*

MIRE BEASTS
These carnivorous monsters were driven underground by the inhospitable climate of the planet Aridius. They multiplied rapidly, feeding on the Aridians who were compelled to constantly blow up the areas of their subterranean city infested by the beasts.

THE CHASE
See also *Aridius*

MISTFALL
The planet Alzarius periodically undergoes a slight orbital shift, cooling the planet and thus producing Mistfall. At this time giant spiders hatch from the river fruits and the Marshmen rise from the swamps, striking terror into the hearts of the Alzarians.

FULL CIRCLE
See also *Alzarius, Marshmen*

MOLYBDENUM
This precious metal was abundant on the Sense Sphere where the Sensorites, once abused by greedy humans, kept its presence secret.

THE SENSORITES
See also *Sensorites*

MONARCH
This froglike Urbankan had kidnapped samples of humanity throughout its history, intending to use them in his plans to conquer Earth. Monarch had destroyed his own planet in obsessive experiments to confirm his suspicion that he was God, his ultimate aim being to travel back in time to the creation and meet himself. His theory was never proved as Adric threw a bottle of deadly poison at him, reducing him to a small green blob.

FOUR TO DOOMSDAY
See also *Bigon, Enlightenment, Persuasion, Urbankans*

MONDAS
Mondas, the tenth planet, was the home of the Cybermen who attempted to drain power from Mondas's twin planet Earth, but destroyed Mondas instead. After this encounter with the Cybermen, the first Doctor regenerated.

THE TENTH PLANET
See also *Cybermen*

MONITOR
This old friend of the Doctor and leader of Logopolis perished when the Master brought about the destruction of Logopolis.

LOGOPOLIS
See also *Logopolis*

MONOIDS
One-eyed slaves of the humans aboard the Ark travelling to Refusis, they eventually became the dominant race, the humans having been contaminated and weakened by Dodo's cold. The two species were eventually persuaded to co-exist peacefully on Refusis.

THE ARK
See also *Ark*

MORBIUS
Morbius, a dictatorial figure on the High Council of the Time Lords, was rejected when he attempted to incite his people to global domination. The embittered Time Lord raised a vast army which, lured by the promise of the Elixir of Life, wreaked havoc throughout the universe, until they were defeated by the Time Lords on Karn. Despite his public execution, the brain of Morbius survived, preserved in nutrients by Solon who furtively constructed a body and braincase in which to house it. Morbius' weakened brain was destroyed in a mindbending contest with the Doctor who collapsed and almost died from the strain.

THE BRAIN OF MORBIUS
See also *Karn, Morbius Monster, Solon*

MORBIUS MONSTER
This grisly hybrid was constructed by Solon as a body for Morbius, and comprised of various parts of unfortunate aliens, including a huge claw, a plastic braincase and the arm of Condo, Solon's servant. Recovering from near strangulation by the homicidal monster, Solon reconnected the brain but, despite his modifications, the creature was again driven mad and eventually forced over a cliff to its death by the Sisterhood of Karn.

THE BRAIN OF MORBIUS
See also *Morbius, Sisterhood, Solon*

MORESTRA
A survey team from the vast Morestran empire landed on Zeta Minor where all but Professor Sorenson perished. The relief party narrowly avoided a similar fate.

PLANET OF EVIL
See also *Sorenson, Zeta Minor*

MORGUS
Morgus, the head of the powerful Spectrox conglomerate, manipulated the political situation on Androzani Major and Minor to increase his own wealth and standing. After murdering the President, Morgus was deposed by his own equally devious subordinate, Timmin, and was subsequently killed by his vengeful enemy, Sharaz Jek.

THE CAVES OF ANDROZANI
See also *Sharaz Jek, Spectrox*

MOROK EMPIRE
The oppressive Morok empire maintained a space museum on Xeros in

which the Doctor and his companions narrowly avoided becoming exhibits. They were rescued by the revolt of the Xerons who defeated the Moroks.

THE SPACE MUSEUM

MORPHOTON
The Morphoton city was controlled by the Morphos, four huge brains encased in glass cases. Using the Mesmatron Machine they brainwashed human slaves who experienced their squalid reality as luxurious illusions. Barbara narrowly escaped strangulation at the hands of a hypnotised Ian by smashing the Morphos' life support systems, freeing her friends from the malignant influence of the city.

THE KEYS OF MARINUS

MOVELLANS
Although humanoid in appearance, the Movellans were ruthless androids, whose total reliance on logic had brought them to an impasse in their protracted war with the equally logical Daleks. The Doctor, blackmailed into reprogramming their computer to defeat the Daleks, succeeded, with the aid of Tyssan, in de-activating all the Movellans on Skaro.

DESTINY OF THE DALEKS
See also *Daleks, Tyssan*

MUMMIES
The ponderous but deadly mummies were in reality heavily-bandaged service robots used by Sutekh.

PYRAMIDS OF MARS
See also *Sutekh*

MUTANTS
The disfiguring insect-like mutation afflicting the humanoid natives of Solos was, unbeknown to them, a stage in their natural cyclical metamorphosis into beautiful super-beings.

THE MUTANTS
See also *Ky, Solos*

MUTOS
A derogatory term given by the Kaleds to the genetically-wounded members of their own race, who were expelled from the city to roam the wastelands.

GENESIS OF THE DALEKS
See also *Kaleds, Sevrin*

MYRKA
The large cumbersome sea-going Cyborg was bred by the Silurians as an offensive weapon. Having infiltrated Sea Base Four the marine monster was despatched by a heavy dose of ultra violet light.

WARRIORS OF THE DEEP
See also *Silurians*

NEEVA

A member of the Sevateem and fanatical priest of Xoanon. Incensed by the Doctor's revelation that Xoanon had deceived him, Neeva attempted to destroy the computer but was himself disintegrated.

THE FACE OF EVIL
See also *Sevateem, Xoanon*

NERO

This decadent Roman emperor amorously pursued Barbara and eventually set fire to the city of Rome.

THE ROMANS

NERVA

Nerva, originally conceived as a space beacon, was attacked by the Cybermen who utilised it in their attempted destruction of Voga. The Doctor had visited Nerva later in its history when, with the threatened extermination of life on Earth by solar flares, it had been converted into a Space Ark. The human passengers, cryogenically suspended, awaited a time when the Earth would once more become habitable, but while they slept a Wirrn invaded the ark, laying her eggs in one of the unfortunate humans. The Doctor alerted the crew to the danger and helped them defeat the Wirrn and return to Earth.

THE ARK IN SPACE
REVENGE OF THE CYBERMEN
See also *Voga, Wirrn*

NESBIN

This former Time Lord, leader of the Outsiders (Shobogans), was persuaded by Leela to help the Time Lords defeat the Vardan and Sontaran invasions of Gallifrey.

THE INVASION OF TIME
See also *Shobogans*

NESTENES

The Nestene Consciousness was a disembodied entity whose original form resembled a combination of crab and octopus. It possessed an affinity with plastic through which the Autons were fashioned, controlled by individual portions of the central brain. The Doctor defeated both attempted invasions, on the second occasion with the aid of the Master who had reactivated the small globe which summoned the Nestene to Earth.

SPEARHEAD FROM SPACE
TERROR OF THE AUTONS
See also *Autons*

NILSON

A saboteur aboard Seabase Four who contrived to initiate a war between two rival Earth powers. He was killed by a Sea Devil warrior.

WARRIORS OF THE DEEP
See also *Myrka, Solow*

NIMON

Although resembling the supposedly mythical Minotaur, these black bull-headed monsters were actually a technologically advanced race who existed by draining planets of their energy, having first seduced the native population with promises of power. In the centre of a maze on Skonnos the Nimon utilised the tributes of Hymetusite to transport his fellows from the ravaged planet of Crinoth to Skonnos where they perished in an explosion.

THE HORNS OF NIMON
See also *Crinoth, Hymetusite, Skonnos*

NOAH
Resurrected after thousands of years of cryogenic suspension, Noah, commander of Space Ark Nerva, became contaminated by, and gradually mutated into, a Wirrn. Momentarily recovering his lost humanity, Noah led the swarm of Wirrn into a trap. He perished with the Wirrn in the ensuing explosion but saved the Ark.

THE ARK IN SPACE
See also *Nerva, Wirrn*

NOVA DEVICE
An immensely powerful bomb with which the Movellans intended to destroy Skaro.

DESTINY OF THE DALEKS
See also *Movellans*

N-SPACE
Normal space is the universe in which the Doctor usually travels, as opposed to E-Space in which he was temporarily trapped. It was maintained beyond its natural point of collapse by a CVE created by the Logopolitans.

See also *CVE, Logopolis*

NUCLEUS
The Nucleus of the Swarm, a microscopic parasitic virus feeding on intellectual activity, infected several humans before finally lodging in the brain of the Doctor. Escaping from destruction through the Doctor's tear duct, the inadvertently-enlarged Nucleus arrived on Titan Base to spawn, where it and its brood were blown up by the Doctor.

THE INVISIBLE ENEMY
See also *Marius*

NYDER

Security commander Nyder, Davros's pathologically cold-hearted assistant, contributed to the destruction of his own race, the Kaleds. He was exterminated by the Daleks whilst obeying Davros's orders.

GENESIS OF THE DALEKS
See also *Daleks, Davros, Kaleds*

NYSSA

The sensitive, aristocratic daughter of Tremas became a companion of the Doctor under traumatic circumstances, her father, stepmother and home planet Traken having been destroyed by the Master. Transported by the Watcher to Logopolis, she joined the crew of the TARDIS, where her naivety and goodness endeared her to Adric and Tegan but also made her particularly susceptible to evil. Outrage at the ordeals suffered by the Lazars on Terminus led Nyssa to remain there, using her considerable technological and bioelectronic skills to cure the Lazars and the Vanir.

THE KEEPER OF TRAKEN – TERMINUS
See also *Terminus, Traken, Tremas, Vanir*

ODYSSEUS

This Greek hero and king of Ithaca, sceptical of the Doctor's validity as Zeus, challenged him to devise a means of entry to Troy. The Doctor suggested a wooden horse.

THE MYTH MAKERS

OGRI

Three of these powerful bloodsucking silicon-based life forms were transported by Cessair of Diplos from their inhospitable planet Ogros (in the Tau Ceti star system) to the planet Earth, where they were disguised as standing stones.

THE STONES OF BLOOD
See also *Cessair, Megara*

OGRONS

These physically intimidating ape-like beings of limited intelligence inhabited a bleak rocky planet where they lived in fear of carnivorous worm-like creatures. Their stupidity and strength made them perfect servants of the Daleks, who used them to police the conquered Earth and, with the Master's aid, to trap the Doctor.

DAY OF THE DALEKS
FRONTIER IN SPACE

OHICA

Maren's subordinate in the Sisterhood, she persuaded her superior to help the

Doctor, leading an attack on the Morbius Monster and becoming high priestess of the sacred flame following Maren's death.

THE BRAIN OF MORBIUS
See also *Maren, Morbius Monster, Sisterhood*

OK CORRAL
The scene of a famous gunfight between the Earps and Clantons in Tombstone, America in 1881.

THE GUNFIGHTERS
See also *Earp*

OLVIR
This inexperienced young space raider landed with Kari on Terminus where he struggled against his initial terror of Lazar disease, from which his sister had perished, to save Nyssa.

TERMINUS
See also *Kari, Terminus*

OMEGA
One of the greatest heroes of Time Lord history. The Omega legend states that this brilliant solar engineer sacrificed himself in the detonation of a star, thus creating the initial power source for time travel. Omega survived, however, dragged through a black hole into the world of anti-matter which he sustained by pure willpower. Embittered by his lonely existence, he projected a light beam through the black hole and began draining energy from Gallifrey which he ultimately intended to rule or destroy. The three Doctors dispatched by the Time Lords to defeat Omega eventually

succeeded, creating a massive explosion by bringing him into contact with the second Doctor's recorder, the only object in his universe not composed of anti-matter. They had discovered that beneath his protective mask nothing of Omega remained but his will, his body having been totally consumed by anti-matter. Their assumption that Omega perished was however premature. Aided by the deluded Time Lord Hedin, Omega almost succeeded in bonding with the fifth Doctor and stealing his body to return to Gallifrey.

THE THREE DOCTORS
ARC OF INFINITY
See also *Anti-matter, Hedin*

OPERATION GOLDEN AGE
Conceived by cabinet minister Sir Charles Grover and Professor Whittaker, inventor of the Time Scoop, the ultimate aim of this secret operation was to return the world to a time period before industrialisation, effectively terminating contemporary life on Earth. Captain Yates was suspended from UNIT due to his part in the operation.

INVASION OF THE DINOSAURS
See also *Time Scoop*

OPTERA
These shrunken caterpillar-like creatures inhabited the tunnels beneath Vortis, hostile towards intruders and unaware of their heritage as Menoptera. Encouraged by Ian and Vrestin they burrowed to the surface of their planet to fight the Animus.

THE WEB PLANET
See also *Animus, Menoptera, Vortis, Vrestin*

ORACLE
The Oracle, keeper of the race banks of Minyos, was a computer which had assumed a godlike identity aboard the disabled P7E, enslaving the Trogs with the aid of its ruthless servants, the Seers. The Oracle was destroyed by the Doctor.

UNDERWORLD
See also *P7E, Seers, Trogs*

ORGANON
Lady Adrasta's court astrologer, he was cast into the pit with Erato following an unpopular prediction, but survived to be rescued by the Doctor.

CREATURE FROM THE PIT
See also *Adrasta, Erato*

OSEIDON
The planet of the Kraals had been riddled with radiation and devastated by a series of atomic wars. As a prelude to the conquest of Earth, a replica English village was created on Oseidon, peopled with android copies of humans. Although initially confused, the Doctor discovered the deception and foiled the invasion.

THE ANDROID INVASION
See also *Kraals*

OSIRIANS
Led by Horus, the brother of Sutekh, this race of superbeings spread throughout the universe where, because of their awesome mental and technological powers, they were worshipped as gods.

PYRAMIDS OF MARS
See also *Phaester Osiris, Sutekh*

OUTLERS
A group of rebellious Alzarian youngsters who, led by Adric's brother Varsh, had absconded from the authority of the Starliner to live in a cave on the planet's surface. Adric was stealing river fruits, an initiation test to join the Outlers, when Mistfall began.

FULL CIRCLE
See also *Adric, Mistfall, Starliner, Varsh*

P7E
Prior to the annihilation of Minyos the spaceship P7E was dispatched to Minyos Two, equipped with a sophisticated computer, Oracle, bearing the race banks of the Minyan people. A planet formed around the P7E, damaged on the edge of the universe, and there it was discovered 100,000 years later by Jackson and his crew, who recovered the race banks. The P7E was accidentally destroyed by the megalomaniac Oracle.

UNDERWORLD
See also *Oracle*

PADMASAMBHAVA
An ancient Tibetan lama and old friend of the Doctor, his body was taken over and used to co-ordinate the Yeti attacks at the Det-Sen monastery. The Doctor defeated the Great Intelligence controlling the lama, allowing the old monk to die in peace.

THE ABOMINABLE SNOWMAN
See also *Great Intelligence, Yeti*

PANGOL
Pangol was the only child of the Tachyon Recreation Generator, created from living cells donated by the Argolin. Having deposed Mena, he attempted to clone an army of warlike Pangols, but was defeated by the Doctor and inadvertently

rejuvenated in the generator, emerging as a harmless baby.

THE LEISURE HIVE
See also *Argolis, Mena, Tachyon Recreation Generator*

PANNA
The wise old woman of the Kinda who revealed to the 'idiot' Doctor the history of the Mara on Deva Loka. When she died, her spirit passed to her protégée Karuna.

KINDA
See also *Kinda, Mara*

PANOPTICON
This great hall at the centre of the Capitol on Gallifrey is the venue for Time Lord rituals and ceremonies. Beneath the Panopticon is housed the Eye of Harmony, the source of power on Gallifrey.

See also *Eye of Harmony, Gallifrey*

PARRINIUM
Found on Exxilon and the antidote to a deadly space plague, it was coveted by both humans and Daleks, who went to war over its possession.

DEATH TO THE DALEKS
See also *Exxilon*

PELADON
This young progressive king of Peladon, a relatively primitive planet, gained admission to the Galactic Federation with the Doctor's aid. Returning in the rule of King Peladon's daughter, Thalira, the Doctor foiled a plot led by Eckersley and the Ice Warriors to invade the planet and seize its valuable trisilicate mines.

THE MONSTER OF PELADON
THE CURSE OF PELADON
See also *Aggedor, Federation, Hepesh, Ice Warriors, Trisilicate*

PERPUGILLIAM BROWN
Peri, a bored young American student holidaying in Lanzarote, found herself in the alien environment of the TARDIS when she was rescued from drowning by Turlough. Despite his warning of the Doctor's propensity for trouble, and an early confrontation with the Master, Peri decided to spend her remaining three months' vacation aboard the TARDIS.

PLANET OF FIRE –

PERSUASION
He and his colleague Enlightenment were Urbankans aboard Monarch's ship, whose mental identity was retained on microchips within an android body. Originally revealing themselves in their natural frog-like form, they soon reappeared in human bodies and clothing startlingly similar to sketches supplied by Tegan. Both Enlightenment and Persuasion perished in a fight against Adric and the Doctor.

FOUR TO DOOMSDAY
See also *Enlightenment, Monarch, Urbankans*

PHAESTER OSIRIS
The planet of the Osirians, it was destroyed by Sutekh as his first step in destroying all sentient life.

PYRAMIDS OF MARS
See also *Osirians, Sutekh*

PHAROS PROJECT
An Earth computer project designed to transmit messages to remote planets through a radio telescope. It was perfectly reproduced on Logopolis, where the Logopolitans ran the program which preserved the universe from entropy. As Logopolis disintegrated, the Doctor and the Master transferred the program to the Pharos Project computer on Earth where the Doctor, having saved the universe, was thrown from the telescope by the Master, and forced to regenerate.

LOGOPOLIS
See also *Logopolis*

PING-CHO
A Chinese girl travelling with Marco Polo to an arranged marriage at the court of Kublai Khan. Befriending Susan, she helped the Doctor against Tegana.

MARCO POLO
See also *Tegana*

PLANTAGENET
With the demise of Captain Revere, commander of Frontios, the uneasy burden of leadership fell upon his son Plantagenet. Although dedicated and aware of the colonists' dependence upon him, Plantagenet appeared temperamentally unsuited to his role until his capture by the Tractators. He emerged from this traumatic experience a stronger, more composed and confident leader.

FRONTIOS
See also *Frontios, Tractators*

PLASMATONS
These amorphous and inanimate particles or protoplasm, bonded by psychic energy, were created by the Xeraphin. Having dominated the dark side of their nature, the Master partly controlled the Plasmatons.

TIME-FLIGHT
See also *Xeriphas*

PLUTO
The planet on which the Usurians established a colony of oppressed Earthpeople, who worked as slaves for the company under Pluto's six artificial suns.

THE SUNMAKERS
See also *Company*

POLLY
Polly, a trendy Londoner working for a computer expert, became involved with the Doctor in his battle against WOTAN who had hypnotised her. Accidentally entering the TARDIS with Ben, she became a companion of the Doctor and witnessed his first regeneration. After the Chameleon invasion she and Ben bid farewell to Jamie and the Doctor, remaining in twentieth-century England.

THE WAR MACHINES – THE FACELESS ONES
See also *Ben, WOTAN*

PORTREEVE
A disguise adopted by the Master to lure the newly regenerated Doctor into Castrovalva's recursive trap.

CASTROVALVA
See also *Castrovalva, Recursive Occlusion*

PRALIX
A psychic inhabitant of the planet Zanak, he became a Mentiad and helped the Doctor to defeat the Captain and Queen Xanxia

THE PIRATE PLANET
See also *Mentiads*

PRIMITIVES
The Primitives, regressives from a once great civilisation, inhabited an underground city on the planet Exarius where they worshipped and made sacrifice to the Guardian.

COLONY IN SPACE
See also *Exarius, Guardian*

PRIMORDS
The Primords were the human victims of a

highly contagious mutating disease, transmitted from contact with a green slime seeping from Project Inferno. Extreme heat transformed the infected, mad, hairy humans into full Primords – powerful bestial wolfmen.

INFERNO
See also *Inferno, Stahlman*

PRYDONIANS
The Time Lord aristocracy is divided into various hierarchies of which the Prydonians, in their scarlet and gold ceremonial gowns, are the most famous. This chapter has provided more Presidents than any other and its members, including Borusa, Goth and the Doctor are noted for their deviousness.

See also *Borusa, Goth*

PYRAMIDS OF MARS
A structure on Mars housing and protecting the Eye of Horus. The Doctor solved a complex series of deadly puzzles to gain entry.

PYRAMIDS OF MARS
See also *Eye of Horus*

QUARKS
The Dominators' small and deadly atomic powered robots, who assisted in the drilling operations on Dulkis. They perished with their masters.

THE DOMINATORS
See also *Dominators*

R

RAAGA
The tinclavic mines of the planet Raaga became a penal colony on which the Terileptil leader sustained disfiguring burns before his escape to Earth.

THE VISITATION
See also *Terileptils*

RAGO
The ruthless leader of the Dominators on Dulkis.

THE DOMINATORS
See also *Dominators*

RANDOMISER
A device fitted by the Doctor to the guidance system of the TARDIS, randomising its co-ordinates and thus denying the Doctor and the Black Guardian prior knowledge of its destination. The Doctor accidentally dropped and shattered the contraption inside the Leisure Hive.

THE ARMAGEDDON FACTOR – THE LEISURE HIVE
See also *Black Guardian*

RANQUIN
The leader of the Swampies and devotee of Kroll. He sentenced the Doctor and Romana to death by the seventh holy ritual, but perished instead in the tentacles of Kroll.

THE POWER OF KROLL
See also *Kroll, Swampies*

RANGE
Mr Range the Chief Science Officer on Frontios and his daughter Norna helped the Doctor discover the subterranean reason for the unaccountable deaths and frequent meteorite showers menacing the planet.

FRONTIOS
See also *Frontios, Gravis, Tractators*

RANSOME, THEA
An innocent scientist involved in Fendleman's time experiments who was possessed and eventually transmuted into the Fendahl core. The creature she had become died in the implosion of Fetch Priory.

IMAGE OF THE FENDAHL
See also *Fendahl*

RASSILON
An almost mythical figure in ancient Time Lord history. The Book of the Old Time states that Rassilon, the first Time Lord, journeyed into a black hole, capturing and stabilising its energies within the Eye of Harmony, which became the power source of Gallifrey and the key to time travel. Rassilon also created the original force fields around Gallifrey and the symbols of presidential power, the Great Key, Sash, Rod and Matrix. The legend also tells, in records preserved in old TARDISes (such as the Doctor's), of his victory over the Great Vampire army. A potentially darker side to his character emerged in the contradictions surrounding the bloodthirsty duels fought in the Death Zone, sometimes referred to as 'the Game of Rassilon'. Official Time Lord history states that he put an end to the

Game, but other legends hold that he in fact initiated it. Rassilon's Tomb lies in the Dark Tower at the centre of the Death Zone on Gallifrey. Few have ever survived to reach it and claim their reward of immortality, and those that have endure a living death trapped in stone upon his tomb. Such was the wisdom of Rassilon.

See also *Eye of Harmony, Gallifrey*

RECOVERY SEVEN
This space ship made two journeys to recover the missing Earth astronauts of Mars Probe Seven. The first resulted in the secret delivery of three alien ambassadors to Earth. The second, piloted by the Doctor, discovered the astronauts safe in the care of the friendly aliens.

THE AMBASSADORS OF DEATH

RECURSIVE OCCLUSION
A phenomenon wherein space folds continuously in on itself. The Doctor was lured into this space-time trap by the Master on Castrovalva.

CASTROVALVA
See also *Castrovalva*

REFUSIS
The planet of the invisible Refusians on which the Human and Monoid occupants of the space Ark finally settled.

THE ARK
See also *Ark, Monoids*

REUBEN
A superstitious lighthouse keeper of Fang Rock. He was killed by the Rutan, his lifeless body being copied and possessed to deadly effect.

HORROR OF FANG ROCK
See also *Fang Rock, Rutans*

REYNART, PRINCE
The rightful king of Tara who was wounded and imprisoned by Count Grendel. The prince eventually acceded to the throne with the aid of a replica android.

THE ANDROIDS OF TARA
See also *Grendel, Tara*

RIBOS
A relatively primitive snow-covered planet of the Cyrrenic Alliance which Garron attempted to sell to the Graff Vynda Ka. The Doctor discovered the first segment of the Key to Time on Ribos.

THE RIBOS OPERATION
See also *Garron, Graff Vynda Ka, Key to Time*

RICHARD THE LIONHEART
Richard I, king of England and France, was encountered by the Doctor on the Crusades in twelfth-century Palestine. Ian was knighted by him, becoming Sir Ian, Knight of Jaffa, whilst the Doctor became involved in court intrigue between Richard and his sister Joanna.

THE CRUSADE
See also *Saladin*

RILLS
Although a gentle and peaceful race, the

Rills were physically unprepossessing creatures resembling tusked warthogs. The Doctor helped them escape from a doomed planet and the warlike Drahvins.

GALAXY FOUR
See also *Drahvins*

ROBOMEN
Humans, irreversibly converted into brainless guards, executing the will of the Daleks on the conquered Earth. The Doctor reprogrammed them to attack the Daleks.

THE DALEK INVASION OF EARTH

ROBOT, GIANT
Created by Professor Kettlewell from living metal, the Robot was originally programmed to utilise its immense physical powers in the service of mankind. Miss Winters tampered with its circuits, however, overriding its primary function, and ordering the mechanically-distressed creature to kill. Having accidentally destroyed its creator, the mentally unstable Robot kidnapped Sarah who had shown it sympathy and went on the rampage, enlarged to gigantic proportions by the startled Brigadier. The Doctor reluctantly disintegrated the misused Robot with a metal viral solution.

ROBOT
See also *Disintegrator Gun, Kettlewell, Winters*

ROBOT, MINING
The remote-controlled IMC mining robot was equipped with lethal claws to terrify

the colonists of Exarius into abandoning their planet. The Doctor almost became one of its victims.

COLONY IN SPACE
See also *IMC*

ROBOT, RASTON
The third Doctor and Sarah were menaced by a Raston Warrior robot in the Death Zone on Gallifrey. Humanoid in form, this shiny, metallic, faceless robot was an immensely agile killing machine. It reacted at the slightest sound with lightning reflexes, destroying a group of Cybermen with deadly javelins and discs released from its fingertips.

THE FIVE DOCTORS

ROBOT, SERVICE
Aboard the Sandminer were three categories of humanoid robots: the speechless Dums who performed the menial tasks, the more sophisticated multi-functional, talking Vocs, and the elite intelligent Super-Vocs. Reprogrammed by Taren Capel, the Robots set about killing their human masters.

THE ROBOTS OF DEATH
See also *Sandminer, Taren Capel*

ROBOT, SERVO
This small efficient Robot attacked the Doctor and Jamie aboard a seemingly abandoned cargo ship, which carried more sinister passengers – the Cybermen. The robot was destroyed by Jamie.

THE WHEEL IN SPACE

ROBOT, WHITE
The terrifying White Robots hunted Jamie and Zoe through a featureless void in the Land of Fiction.

THE MIND ROBBER

RODAN
A female Time Lord who, bored with her galactic traffic control duties, escaped from the Capitol with Leela to help the Shobogans repel the alien invasion of Gallifrey.

THE INVASION OF TIME
See also *Gallifrey, Shobogans*

ROHM DUTT
A gun-runner in the pay of Thawn, he sold defective arms to the Swampies and was killed by Kroll.

THE POWER OF KROLL
See also *Kroll, Swampies, Thawn*

ROMANA
The proud, aristocratic Lady Romanadvoratrelundar was dispatched by the White Guardian to help the Doctor recover the Key to Time. A recent graduate of the Time Lord Academy, her original attitude towards the Doctor was one of haughty tolerance which rapidly changed to respect. The Doctor, though initially piqued by her uninvited presence aboard his TARDIS, soon warmed to his intelligent Time Lady companion. Having disposed of the Key to Time, Romana regenerated into the likeness of Princess Astra, adopting a carefree, fun-loving outlook on life, more in tune with the

attitude of the fourth Doctor. Dreading her return to the restrictions of Gallifrey, Romana elected to remain in E-Space with K9 and help the Tharils rebuild a just society.

THE RIBOS OPERATION – WARRIORS' GATE
See also *Astra, Key to Time, Tharils*

RORVIK
The implacable commander of a slave ship trapped in E-Space. He forced the time-sensitive Tharil slaves and the captured Romana to visualise, an excruciatingly traumatic mode of navigation. Rorvik died in an explosion engendered by an attempt to blast his ship out of E-Space.

WARRIORS' GATE
See also *Tharils*

RUBEISH, PROFESSOR
An endearingly absent-minded professor who was transported by Linx from twentieth-century England to the Middle Ages. The Doctor returned him, along with his fellow scientists, to their correct time period.

THE TIME WARRIOR
See also *Linx, Sontarans*

RUMFORD, PROFESSOR AMELIA
An eccentric old professor of ancient history and unsuspecting friend of Vivien Fay, she helped the Doctor to unravel the mystery surrounding the Stones of Blood.

THE STONES OF BLOOD
See also *Cessair of Diplos, Ogri*

RUTANS
An amorphous semi-transparent warlike race from the icy planet of Ruta Three, they recharge on electricity and have the ability to adopt the form of other beings. Their attempted conquest of Earth, which they intended to use as a pawn in their interminable war against the Sontarans, was prevented by the Doctor who blew up the Rutan scout and invasion fleet on Fang Rock.

HORROR OF FANG ROCK
See also *Fang Rock, Sontarans*

S

SALADIN
This chivalrous, all-powerful Moslem ruler opposed King Richard I of England during the Third Crusade.

THE CRUSADE
See also *Richard the Lionheart*

SALAMANDER
Beneath Salamander's benevolent public image lurked a shrewd, totally immoral politician. Bent upon world dictatorship, he utilised his invention, the Sunstore, to create a series of apparently natural catastrophes to further his own ambitions. The second Doctor, bearing a striking resemblance to the potential dictator, impersonated Salamander, but was himself impersonated by the politician who thus gained entry to the TARDIS. In attempting to operate the TARDIS whilst the doors remained open, Salamander was sucked into space.

ENEMY OF THE WORLD
See also *Kent*

SALATEEN
A replica android of the young Major Salateen had been substituted by Sharaz Jek who held the true Salateen captive. Having eventually escaped, Salateen was killed by androids whilst his copy was immobilised during its futile attempt to save the life of its master, Sharaz Jek.

THE CAVES OF ANDROZANI
See also *Chellak, Sharaz Jek*

SALYAVIN
A notoriously brilliant Time Lord criminal who, having escaped from imprisonment on Shada, retired secretly to Earth,

adopting the pseudonym of Professor Chronotis. The evil Skagra sought Salyavin's mental abilities, the possession of which would enable him to project his thoughts into the minds of others. Having defeated Skagra with the Doctor's aid, Salyavin returned to Earth and resumed his life as Professor Chronotis.

SHADA
See also *Chronotis, Shada, Skagra*

SANDERS
The imperialistic, though basically good-natured, commander of the survey party on Deva Loka. He recovered from a temporary lapse into childlike insanity induced by the Box of Jana, and reported that Deva Loka was unsuitable for colonisation.

KINDA
See also *Deva Loka*

SANDMINER
Several unexplained fatalities had occurred aboard the Sandminer, a huge mobile mining machine inhabited by lackadaisical robot-dependent humans and their mechanical servants. Virtually the entire crew perished before the Doctor, a prime suspect, could convince the terrified humans of the true identity of the murderers.

THE ROBOTS OF DEATH
See also *Taren Capel*

SAN MARTINO
A small Italian province which was temporarily invaded by the Mandragora Helix during the Renaissance. The Doctor helped the rightful heir, Giuliano, to recover the dukedom from his scheming uncle and Mandragora.

THE MASQUE OF MANDRAGORA
See also *Giuliano, Hieronymous*

SARA KINGDOM
Sara, a dedicated space agent for Mavic Chen, was the sister of Bret Vyon whom she killed. Once alerted to Chen's treachery she became a companion, aiding the Doctor against the Daleks and ultimately perishing, aged to death in seconds by the Time Destructor.

THE DALEK MASTER PLAN
See also *Chen, Vyon*

SARAH JANE SMITH
This independent and resourceful young journalist first encountered the Doctor whilst impersonating her aunt, Lavinia Smith, the famous virologist, in a ploy to gain access to a top secret scientific establishment. Aggravated by the Doctor's apparently chauvanistic attitude towards her and suspecting his implication in the disappearance of several scientists, she stowed away aboard the TARDIS and was transported back to medieval England in the first of her numerous adventures with the Doctor. Having witnessed his third regeneration, she resumed her travels with the fourth Doctor, accompanied for a while by Harry Sullivan. Sarah Jane's long association with the Doctor came to an abrupt end when he was urgently summoned to Gallifrey, so necessitating Sarah's immediate return to Earth. He never forgot her, however, and

Anti-clockwise from top: Doctor Solon, Styre the Sontaran, Professor Sorensen and Salamander, the second Doctor's double.

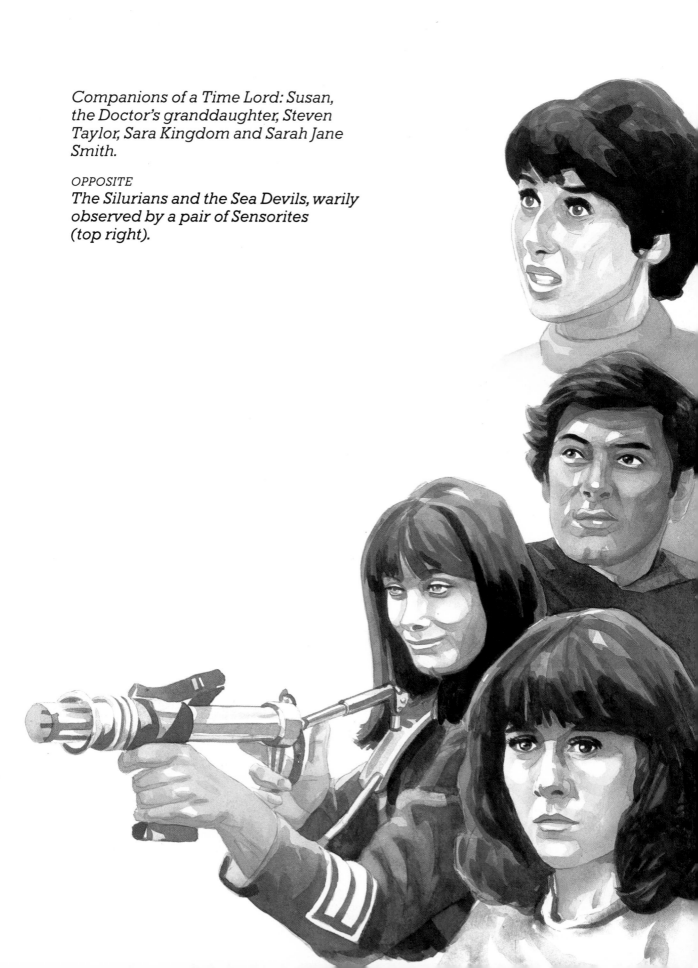

Companions of a Time Lord: Susan, the Doctor's granddaughter, Steven Taylor, Sara Kingdom and Sarah Jane Smith.

OPPOSITE
The Silurians and the Sea Devils, warily observed by a pair of Sensorites (top right).

The robot SV7, Sarah Jane Smith and Mr. Sin, the Peking Homunculus, watched over by the awesome figure of Sutekh the Destroyer.

sent her an unusual gift, K9 Mark 3.

Sarah Jane might never have set eyes on the Doctor again had she heeded the advice of her mechanical hound but, paradoxically, she became involved in a plot with all five Doctors and was thus reunited with the Doctor as she had first known him.

THE TIME WARRIOR – THE FIVE DOCTORS; also K9 AND COMPANY
See also *Harry Sullivan*

SARN
A barren volcanic world and former Trion prison colony. The ancient superstitions of the community were perpetuated by Timanov but faced increasing opposition from the younger elements led by Amyand. The arrival of the Master seeking the sacred volcano's restorative gases necessitated the evacuation of the entire population to their ancestral home – Trion.

PLANET OF FIRE
See also *Logar, Timanov, Trion*

SAVAGES
A race of apparently Stone Age culture, they were misused by their fellow inhabitants, the advanced Elders, who transferred the Savages' life force to themselves, leaving the former depleted and drained.

THE SAVAGES
See also *Elders*

SAVANTS
The scientific and technological caste of Tigellan society. Their demands for scientific analysis of the Dodecahedron brought them into permanent opposition to the Deons.

MEGLOS
See also *Deons*

SCARLIONI
A pseudonym adopted by one of the splinters of Scaroth's personality, cast adrift in twentieth-century France. Count Scarlioni was responsible for the Paris time slips and the murder of his wife when she discovered his true identity.

CITY OF DEATH
See also *Jagaroth, Scaroth*

SCARMAN, MARCUS
Upon discovering the pyramid of Sutekh in 1911, the egyptologist, Marcus Scarman, was consumed by the Osirian's malign influence. Reduced to a walking cadaver powered by the will of Sutekh he returned to England, killed his brother Laurence, and almost succeeded in releasing Sutekh from the power of the Eye of Horus. The body which was once Scarman disintegrated when his usefulness ceased.

PYRAMIDS OF MARS
See also *Eye of Horus, Sutekh*

SCAROTH
The explosion of a Jagaroth spaceship on primeval Earth flung Scaroth, last of the Jagaroth, into the time vortex, splintering him into twelve separate, though telepathically-connected personalities. Scattered throughout Earth's history, they guided mankind's technological

development from the wheel to its ultimate aim, Kerensky's time machine. Scaroth attempted to travel back in time and prevent his initial dispersion, but was prevented by the Doctor who realised that the explosion of Scaroth's spaceship had created life on Earth.

CITY OF DEATH
See also *Jagaroth, Kerensky, Scarlioni*

SCOPE
A peepshow containing captured and miniaturised environments the inhabitants of which, including a herd of Drashigs and the crew of the missing *SS Bernice*, unwittingly enacted a continuous repetition of events. The Doctor escaped from the Scope, and succeeded in returning the exhibits to their correct positions in time and space.

CARNIVAL OF MONSTERS
See also *Drashigs, Vorg*

SCORBY
Harrison Chase's sadistic henchman, he stole a Krynoid pod from the Antarctic, leaving devastation in his wake. He died in an attempt to escape from the monster, being dragged beneath the waters by writhing vegetation on Chase's estate.

THE SEEDS OF DOOM
See also *Krynoid*

SCOTT, LIEUTENANT
A hardened squad commander on twenty-sixth-century Earth who stepped aboard the TARDIS to help the Doctor defeat the Cybermen.

EARTHSHOCK

SEA BASE FOUR
This underwater military installation equipped with nuclear weapons, one of many maintaining the balance of power in Earth's future, was attacked simultaneously from two totally unrelated sources. An internal threat was posed by the saboteurs Solow and Nilson, and an external one by the combined forces of Silurians and Sea Devils.

WARRIORS OF THE DEEP
See also *Nilson, Sea Devils, Silurians, Solow*

SEA DEVILS
'Sea Devils' was the name given by humans to the intelligent lizard-like amphibious life forms related to the Silurians. Fearing global devastation from the body which ultimately became Earth's moon, they had retreated into underground hibernation shelters, oversleeping by millions of years whilst their supremacy over the Earth was eclipsed by man. Awoken by drilling operations, a colony of Sea Devils armed with deadly hand guns and aided by the Master set about reclaiming their planet from humanity. In a second attempt to rid their Earth from mankind, another colony of Sea Devil warriors was revived by their Silurian cousins to lead an assault on Sea Base Four. As in their previous encounter a saddened Doctor was ultimately responsible for their annihilation.

THE SEA DEVILS
WARRIORS OF THE DEEP
See also *Sea Base Four, Silurians*

SEERS
These hooded semi-robotised servants of

the Oracle evolved from a section of the surviving Minyans of the P7E. They perished with the Oracle.

UNDERWORLD
See also *P7E*

SENSORITES

A deeply intelligent and civilised telepathic race inhabiting the planet Sense Sphere. Having experienced human exploitation of their molybdenum-rich planet, they held Captain Maitland's crew in semi-somnambulent captivity in orbit around the Sense Sphere. Their harsh policy was revised with the aid of the Doctor, whom they contacted through telepathic messages to Susan.

THE SENSORITES
See also *Maitland, Molybdenum*

SETH

A captive Anethian youth who, out of bravado, swore to kill the Nimon, to whom he had been given as tribute. He and his party were rescued by the Doctor and Romana.

THE HORNS OF NIMON
See also *Nimon*

SEVATEEM

Two feuding tribes, the Tesh and the Sevateem, shared a planet, both tribes oblivious of their mutual ancestry from terrestrial colonists. The primitive and warlike Sevateem (a corruption of the words 'Survey Team') inhabited the jungle, surviving on their wits and instincts and worshipping their god Xoanon. The two tribes were eventually reconciled as a result of the Doctor's intervention. Leela was a member of the Sevateem tribe.

THE FACE OF EVIL
See also *Leela, Tesh, Xoanon*

SEVRIN

Sevrin, a Muto, befriended Sarah in the wastelands of Skaro. Having escaped from their Thal captors, he joined the resistance movement against the Daleks.

GENESIS OF THE DALEKS
See also *Mutos*

SHADA

The infamous penal planet of the Time Lords, all knowledge of which was erased from their memory by Salyavin, an escaped convict of Shada. The Key to the planet's whereabouts was contained within a book *The Ancient Law of Gallifrey* which was stolen from the Panopticon by Salyavin to prevent discovery of his escape.

SHADA
See also *Salyavin*

SHADOW

A sinister cowled servant of the Black Guardian whose asteroid lair floated between Atrios and Zeos, twin planets in the process of destroying each other at his instigation. To procure the Key to Time for his master the Shadow captured Princess Astra, the Doctor, Romana and K9, but perished when his asteroid was accidentally exploded by his pawn, the Marshal.

THE ARMAGEDDON FACTOR
See also *Guardian, Black, Key to Time*

SHARAZ JEK

This masked and mutilated guerilla leader equipped with armed androids fought the troops of the powerful Spectrox conglomerate in the tunnels of Androzani Minor. Morbidly infatuated by Peri's beauty he kidnapped her and the Doctor, saving their lives yet oblivious to their gradual deterioration from spectrox toxaemia. Although fatally wounded by Stotz, Jek survived long enough to kill his hated adversary Morgus, to whom he owed his disfigured features.

THE CAVES OF ANDROZANI
See also *Morgus, Stotz*

SHARREL

The commander of the Movellan mission to Skaro. He was deactivated by Romana whilst attempting to explode the Nova device.

DESTINY OF THE DALEKS
See also *Movellans*

SHIRNA

A showgirl from the planet Lurma who travelled with Vorg and his Scope to entertain the inhabitants of Inter Minor.

CARNIVAL OF MONSTERS
See also *Inter Minor, Scope, Vorg*

SHOBOGANS

The Shobogans or Outsiders were small communities of Gallifreyans (including Time Lords) who, for various reasons, had rejected Time Lord society to live and hunt in primitive conditions on the planet's surface. Leela persuaded a group led by the Time Lord Nesbin to return to the Capitol and oppose the Sontaran invasion.

THE INVASION OF TIME
See also *Nesbin, Sontarans*

SHRIVENZALES

Huge reptilian creatures which guarded the relic chamber and inhabited the catacombs beneath Ribos.

THE RIBOS OPERATION
See also *Ribos*

SHURA

A fanatical guerilla transported, with his comrades, from twenty-second-century Earth back to the twentieth-century to kill Sir Reginald Styles, whom they held responsible for the subsequent Dalek domination of Earth. Shura, discovering that Styles's death had precipitated the Daleks' supremacy, sacrificed his own life in an explosion which destroyed the Daleks, thus altering the Earth's future.

DAY OF THE DALEKS
See also *Styles*

SIDRATS

These TARDIS-like machines, programmed for short hops between the time zones, were procured by the renegade Time Lord, the War Chief, for use in the War Games.

THE WAR GAMES
See also *War Chief*

SILURIANS

Intelligent reptilian relatives of the Sea Devils, possessing a third eye in the centre of their foreheads through which they focussed deadly rays of mental energy. Fearing global devastation from the body which ultimately became Earth's moon, they had retreated into underground hibernation shelters, oversleeping by millions of years whilst their supremacy over the Earth was eclipsed by man. Eventually a small colony beneath Wenley Moor was awakened by the activities of an underground atomic research station. The old Silurian leader supported the Doctor's efforts to negotiate peace between the two races, whilst the more fanatical element attempted to destroy mankind and the Van Allen Belt which protects the Earth from the full force of the sun's rays. To the Doctor's disgust the entire colony was destroyed by the Brigadier. The Silurians, now totally committed to the extinction of Man, revived a colony of Sea Devils and launched a combined attack on an Earth Sea Base. The despairing Doctor was compelled to destroy them with poison gas.

THE SILURIANS
WARRIORS OF THE DEEP
See also *Sea Base Four, Sea Devils*

SIN, MR
The Peking Homunculus, alias Mr Sin, was a robotic assassination machine incorporating a pig's brain and tiny computer and possessing an insane hatred for mankind. Created by Magnus Greel in the year 5,000, it resurfaced in Victorian England masquerading as a Chinese ventriloquist's dummy. The malevolent knife-wielding doll was defused by the Doctor.

THE TALONS OF WENG CHIANG
See also *Weng-Chiang*

SISTERHOOD OF THE FLAME
The Sisterhood guarded and worshipped the Sacred Flame, provider of the Elixir of Life which perpetuated their immortality. Their awesome telekinetic powers drew the TARDIS to Karn where they resided, led by the ancient Maren and her successor, Ohica.

THE BRAIN OF MORBIUS
See also *Elixir of Life, Karn, Maren, Ohica.*

SKAGRA
An alien scientist who, through his floating globes, possessed the ability to steal minds. The megalomaniac's ultimate ambition, however, was to place imprints of his own mind into every sentient being, to achieve which he needed the mind of the Time Lord, Salyavin. The Doctor, recovering from temporary amnesia, trapped Skagra aboard his reprogrammed computerised spaceship.

SHADA
See also *Salyavin*

SKARASEN

See *Loch Ness Monster*

SKARO
This barren irradiated planet gave birth to one of the most evil life forms in the universe, the Daleks. The interminable war of attrition waged between the two native species, the Thals and the Kaleds, devastated the planet's surface, carbonising the vegetation and driving the Daleks underground into subterranean

metallic cities, from which they eventually emerged intent on conquest.

See also *Daleks, Davros, Kaleds, Thals*

SKONNOS
Once the heart of the great Skonnan Empire, this fading militaristic planet was offered renewed power by the Nimon in exchange for regular tributes. The Doctor saved the planet from inevitable extinction by destroying the Nimon's power complex and transmat terminal on Skonnos.

THE HORNS OF NIMON
See also *Nimon, Soldeed*

SKYBASE
An outpost of Earth's empire in the late thirtieth century which, under the command of the sadistic Marshal, ruled the planet Solos. Following his death a temporary marshal was appointed to facilitate Solos' independence.

THE MUTANTS
See also *Marshal, Solos*

SLYTHER
A voracious pet brought from Skaro to Earth by the Black Dalek to guard the Bedfordshire mine. It hurtled to its death down a mine shaft whilst pursuing Ian.

THE DALEK INVASION OF EARTH

SNAKEDANCERS
A largely ignored mystical sect of Manussan society, who retired from society to lead a life of peace and contemplation in their attempts to reach the still point of their minds.

SNAKEDANCE
See also *Manussa*

SOLDEED
The voice of the Nimon on Skonnos. Driven insane as his dreams of power receded, Soldeed attempted to blow up the Nimon's power complex but was killed in the explosion caused by Seth firing Sezom's staff at the controls.

THE HORNS OF NIMON
See also *Skonnos*

SOLE
An old and respected member of the Sevateem. He died bravely whilst taking the test of the Horda, in a futile attempt to save the life of his daughter, Leela, who had blasphemed against Xoanon.

THE FACE OF EVIL
See also *Horda, Leela, Sevateem, Xoanon*

SOLON
Doctor Mehendri Solon, an unprincipled but talented surgeon, became a follower of the cult of Morbius. On the planet Karn, he secretly rescued and preserved the living brain of his criminal master. Solon, having constructed Morbius' powerful hybrid body from pieces of unfortunate aliens, was overjoyed at the Doctor's arrival, desiring his head for the brain case of Morbius. The Doctor, however, avoided this dubious honour by

asphixiating Solon with hydrogen cyanide gas.

THE BRAIN OF MORBIUS
See also *Condo, Karn, Morbius Monster*

SOLOS
Every five hundred years the orbital shift of the planet Solos induces environmental changes which trigger a cyclical metamorphosis in the native Solonians. These warrior tribes, led by war chiefs such as Ky and Varen, feuded against each other, Ky's faction seeking independence from the Earth Empire which ruled Solos from Skybase. The Marshal, commander of Skybase, jeapordised both the planet and its inhabitants by his crazed chemical bombardment of the planet's surface and indiscriminate extermination of the mutant Solonians.

THE MUTANTS
See also *Ky, Mutants, Skybase*

SOLOW
Doctor Solow was Nilson's fellow saboteur on Sea Base Four, who reprogrammed the synch operator Maddox to destroy the base's computer. She was killed by the Myrka.

WARRIORS OF THE DEEP
See also *Myrka, Nilson, Sea Base Four*

SONDERGAARD
This principled Earthman, believed to have been killed by the Marshal, escaped to Solos where he lived with the Mutants in the mines, studying their culture. His knowledge helped the Doctor to unravel the mystery of their mutations.

THE MUTANTS
See also *Mutants*

SONIC SCREWDRIVER
The Doctor's invaluable multi-purpose gadget was first utilised by him in his second incarnation to unscrew an inspection box on a gas pipe. Since then it appeared regularly, its functions varying from radiation detector to laser beam. Romana constructed a more refined version which the Doctor unsuccessfully attempted to substitute for his own. The screwdriver was eventually destroyed by a Terileptil whilst the fifth Doctor struggled to remove an obstinate pair of handcuffs. He commented sadly that it was as if he had lost an old friend.

FURY FROM THE DEEP – THE VISITATION

SONTARANS
A cloned race of intelligent, militaristic beings from the planet Sontara, whose battle fleets waged an interminable war against the equally warlike Rutans. The compact troll-like Sontarans are incredibly powerful and can recharge their energy supplies through the probic vent on the back of their necks – their Achilles heel. The Doctor first encountered a stranded Sontaran officer in medieval England, and another in Earth's distant future, dispassionately torturing human captives to assess their potential resistance to conquest. On

of the anti-matter monster, was diverted from his disastrous research into anti-matter by the Doctor.

PLANET OF EVIL
See also *Anti-matter Monster, Morestra, Zeta Minor*

SPACE MUSEUM
An institution of the Morok Empire, situated on the planet Xeros, in which the Doctor and his companions became lifeless exhibits in a possible alternative future. The museum was destroyed by the liberated Xerons to prevent that future becoming reality.

THE SPACE MUSEUM
See also *Moroks, Xeros*

another occasion a Sontaran battle fleet attempted an invasion of Gallifrey.

THE TIME WARRIOR – THE TWO DOCTORS
See also *Linx, Stor, Styre*

SORENSON
The leader and sole survivor of the original Morestran survey team on Zeta Minor. A dedicated scientist, he collected samples of anti-matter, a potentially revolutionary power source. He became infected by the substance, rapidly losing his sanity and ultimately mutating into an anti-man, a hairy, red-eyed, Neanderthal beast whose touch spelled death. Sorenson, miraculously cured in the pool

SPANDRELL
This tough, cynical commander of the Chancellery Guard helped the Doctor to establish his innocence of the murder of the Time Lord President.

THE DEADLY ASSASSIN

SPECTROX
An invaluable substance found on Androzani Minor with rejuvenating properties, over which Morgus held a monopoly. Contact with Spectrox in its raw web-like state induces Spectrox Toxaemia, the only antidote for which is milk from the queen bat. Exposure to Spectrox precipitated the Doctor's fifth regeneration.

THE CAVES OF ANDROZANI
See also *Androzani, Morgus*

SPIDERS
A malevolent species of giant spider inhabiting the planet Metebelis Three who, abhorring their Earthly origins, adopted the appellation 'Eightlegs'. The original spiders travelled to Metebelis in an Earth spaceship with the human colonists who became their slaves and occasional foodsource. They floated to the Crystal Mountains where their minds and bodies became enlarged and, imbued with telepathic powers, they teleported to Earth, possessing several humans, including Sarah, in their quest to regain the Doctor's crystal. The entire spider colony perished with the death of the Great One.

PLANET OF THE SPIDERS
See also *Great One, Lupton, Metebelis Three*

SPIRIDON
A jungle planet covered in deadly spore-emitting fungi, whose native Spiridons, having perfected invisibility via anti-refractive light waves, were enslaved by the Daleks who also desired invisibility. With the aid of an exploding icecano, the Doctor and a party of Thals refroze a vast Dalek army beneath the planet's surface.

PLANET OF THE DALEKS

STAHLMAN
Professor Stahlman was the brains behind Project Inferno. He hoped to give his name to Earth's new energy source, Stahlman's Gas, but instead became infected with a green slime which transformed him into a Primord.

INFERNO
See also *Inferno, Primords*

STAPLEY
The captain of Concorde Golf Alpha Charlie, who was transported with his jet, crew, and the Doctor to Earth's prehistoric past.

TIME-FLIGHT

STARLINER
For generations the Alzarians living aboard the grounded Starliner had rechecked and replaced perfectly adequate equipment in the mistaken belief that they would eventually return to their home planet Terradon. Only the Chief Decider knew the truth, that on arrival the original Terradonian crew had been massacred by Marshmen from

whom the Alzarians were in fact descended. Having been instructed on the flight procedure by the Doctor, the Starliner finally took off, packed with Alzarians in search of a new home.

FULL CIRCLE
See also *Alzarius, Marshmen*

STEVEN TAYLOR
When the Earth astronaut Steven Taylor crashed on the planet Mechanus, he was cared for by the Mechonoids but held for two years as a virtual prisoner until rescued by the Doctor. Stumbling unnoticed aboard the TARDIS, Steven became a strong-willed companion of the Doctor with whom he had frequent arguments. Following his role in the overthrow of the Elders' unjust regime, Steven was elected by both Elders and Savages to become their leader and help them to build a humane society.

THE CHASE – THE SAVAGES
See also *Elders, Mechonoids, Savages*

STEVENS
The manager of Global Chemicals who, although brainwashed by BOSS, eventually sabotaged and died together with the computer who had become his only friend.

THE GREEN DEATH
See also *BOSS*

STIEN
Stien, apparently a timid refugee from the Daleks, was actually a replica android and Dalek spy. Struggling to reclaim his subjugated identity he released the Doctor and although fatally wounded by the Daleks succeeded in destroying them and the space prison they had occupied.

RESURRECTION OF THE DALEKS

STIRLING, JAMES
Lemaitre, governor of the Conciergerie prison and a high-ranking official in Robespierre's revolutionary government, was secretly the English spy, James Stirling. He attempted to prevent Napoleon's rise to power in France.

THE REIGN OF TERROR

STOR
The commander of the Sontaran battle fleet in the attempted invasion of Gallifrey. The Doctor destroyed him with the De-Mat gun.

THE INVASION OF TIME

STOTZ
A wily unprincipled mercenary who performed shady arms and Spectrox deals with Sharaz Jek. Having murdered his accomplices Stotz accompanied Morgus, his secret employer, to Sharaz Jek's lair where he was shot by the android Salateen.

THE CAVES OF ANDROZANI
See also *Morgus, Salateen, Sharaz Jek*

STRELLA
A royal princess of Tara who eventually became the bride of Prince Reynart. Her

amazing physical resemblance to Romana's first incarnation involved both ladies in Count Grendel's intrigues to gain the throne of Tara.

THE ANDROIDS OF TARA
See also *Grendel, Reynart, Tara*

STRIKER
Adopting the role of a nineteenth-century English sea captain, this emotionally-detached Eternal competed in a bizarre space race between rival sea-going vessels.

ENLIGHTENMENT
See also *Eternals*

STYGGRON
The chief Kraal scientist, and co-ordinator of their proposed invasion of Earth. Having failed to destroy the Doctor and Sarah on Oseidon he perished on Earth, a victim of his own viral solution

THE ANDROID INVASION
See also *Kraals*

STYLES, SIR REGINALD
This respected and dedicated diplomat, presiding over a crucial international peace conference in twentieth-century England, was mistakenly held responsible by twenty-second century guerillas for Earth's future conquest by the Daleks. Having travelled back in time to kill him, they were prevented by the Doctor who revealed that it was their successful assassination of Styles in a previous time which had precipitated the Dalek invasion.

DAY OF THE DALEKS
See also *Shura*

STYRE
On an Earth rendered barren by solar flares a sadistic Sontaran officer, Styre, tortured captive humans, including Sarah, to assess their capacity for resistance.

THE SONTARAN EXPERIMENT

SUSAN FOREMAN
The Doctor's enigmatic grandchild had settled with her exiled grandfather on twentieth-century Earth when her peaceful sojourn at Coal Hill school was abruptly shattered by the misguided intervention of two schoolteachers, Ian Chesterton and Barbara Wright. Compelled to leave Earth with the schoolteachers, the apprehensive and inquisitive adolescent clung to the Doctor through countless adventures until she eventually fell in love with the freedom fighter David Campbell. Realising Susan's inability to desert him, the anguished Doctor locked her out of the TARDIS, leaving her to build a secure future on the newly-liberated Earth. The deadly games of President Borusa briefly reunited the adult Susan with her grandfather and his later selves.

AN UNEARTHLY CHILD – THE FIVE DOCTORS
See also *Barbara, Campbell, Ian*

SUTEKH
Sutekh the Destroyer, a jackal-faced Osirian possessing almost limitless powers, laid waste the galaxy, destroying his own planet Phaester Osiris in his insane hatred for all sentient beings. He was eventually captured by 740 Osirians led by his brother, Horus, and imprisoned beneath a pyramid in ancient Egypt

where, in 1911, he was discovered by
Marcus Scarman. The Doctor trapped his
evil adversary in a space-time tunnel,
propelling him forward 7,000 years to his
death.

PYRAMIDS OF MARS
See also *Eye of Horus, Osirians, Scarman*

SV7
Super Voc 7, the superior service
robot aboard the Sandminer, was
reprogrammed by Taren Capel to
co-ordinate the murder of the human
controllers. Before his demise at the hands
of the Doctor SV7 unknowingly strangled
Taren Capel to death, failing to recognise
his master's voice in the helium-enriched
air.

THE ROBOTS OF DEATH
See also *Taren Capel*

SWAMPIES
The descendants of the natives of Delta
Magna who were transported to Delta
Three. They lived in the marshes,
worshipping Kroll and deeply resenting
the unauthorised presence of the Dryfoots'
methane refinery on their reservation.

THE POWER OF KROLL
See also *Delta Magna, Kroll*

TA
The planet housing the Issigri Mining
Company on which Dom Issigri was held
captive by Caven.

THE SPACE PIRATES
See also *Caven, Issigri*

TACHYON RECREATION GENERATOR
The pride of Argolin technology, it was the
focal point of the Leisure Hive, performing
visual impossibilities such as Pangol's
harmless dismemberment. It was,
however, also capable of giving life –
Pangol was created in the generator and
later, with Mena, rejuvenated.

THE LEISURE HIVE
See also *Leisure Hive, Mena, Pangol*

TALBOT, ANN
Nyssa's virtual double. Her innocent joke
of providing identical costumes for the
two girls at a 1920's masque ball resulted
in Nyssa being kidnapped by Ann's
disfigured former fiancé.

BLACK ORCHID
See also *Cranleigh*

TARA
A rural planet displaying a strange cultural
mix between advanced technology (the
domain of the peasants who fashioned
sophisticated androids, electronic swords
and cross bows for their lords) and the

ancient knightly traditions of the aristocracy, who regarded technological skills as beneath their dignity. Part of a Taran statue proved to be the fourth segment of the Key to Time.

THE ANDROIDS OF TARA
See also *Key to Time, Grendel, Reynart*

TARANIUM CORE

This vital element in the Daleks' Time Destructor was provided by Mavic Chen and stolen by the Doctor, thus initiating a deadly race through time and space, with the Daleks and the Meddling Monk in pursuit.

THE DALEK MASTER PLAN
See also *Chen*

TARDIS

An acronym for Time And Relative Dimensions In Space. A TARDIS is an immensely complex Time Lord study and travel machine. Capable of transporting its operator to any position in time and space, it is dimensionally transcendental and virtually impervious to attack, possessing impenetrable forcefields and the facility to dematerialise out of dangerous situations. As TARDIS design is constantly updated by the Time Lords the Doctor's stolen Type 40 remains the only model of its kind still functioning, albeit somewhat erratically. Access to the Type 40 is via the operator's isomorphic key which only responds to those programmed to use it, though with the Doctor's TARDIS this is not always the case.

TARDISes develop an obscure telepathic affinity with their owners, which perhaps explains the frequently unreliable and temperamental behaviour of the Doctor's ancient, accident-prone machine. Its most obvious malfunction is the chameleon circuit which should transform the exterior appearance of a TARDIS to blend in with its surroundings. The Doctor's machine, however, jammed in Totter's Yard, England, in the 1960s and has since retained the form of a London police telephone box.

The exact size and structure of the TARDIS is variable, as rooms are occasionally jettisoned (as was the Zero Room), but besides the control rooms, of which there are at least two, the ship is known to contain a costume room, endless passageways, a huge swimming pool and a multi-pillared area known as the Cloisters. In the centre of the control room is the heart of the time machine, a six-sided console from which the Doctor, with varying degrees of success, attempts to control his TARDIS.

Other TARDISes encountered by the Doctor include those used by the Meddling Monk, the War Chief and the Master.

See also *Cloister Bell, Dimensionally Transcendental, Sidrats, Time Ring*

TAREN CAPEL

Taren Capel (alias Dask) reprogrammed the robots aboard the Sandminer to slaughter their human masters. Raised amongst robots, the mad scientist believed himself to be one of them. He was accidentally strangled by SV7 who failed to recognise his master's voice which was distorted by the helium-enriched air.

THE ROBOTS OF DEATH
See also *SV7*

TEGAN JOVANKA

This argumentative, self-assured Australian airhostess blundered into the TARDIS after her car broke down on a motorway. She became involved in the Master's confrontation with the Doctor resulting in the latter's fourth regeneration and the murder of Tegan's aunt Vanessa. Tegan's relationship with the Doctor was punctuated by constant criticism of his piloting abilities, although her own attempts to control his erratic machine were proved to be far from perfect.

The recurrence of misfortune and deaths, such as Adric's, which haunt the Doctor's travels, was eventually brought home to Tegan by a bloody encounter with the Daleks and, unwilling to contemplate further journeys in the TARDIS, she decided to remain in twentieth-century England.

LOGOPOLIS – RESURRECTION OF THE DALEKS

TEGANA

A Mongol warlord travelling with Marco Polo to the court of Kublai Khan, ostensibly as a peace emissary, but actually to kill him. Having failed in his mission Tegana committed suicide.

MARCO POLO
See also *Marco Polo*

TELOS

A barren sandy planet housing the remains of an ancient Cybermen city. The former colonists of Telos, frozen in tombs, awaited the advent of humans intelligent enough to revive them. The unfortunate rescuers were then to be converted into Cybermen.

THE TOMB OF THE CYBERMEN
ATTACK OF THE CYBERMEN
See also *Kaftan, Klieg*

TELURIUM

A crystalline substance of which the Krotons and their ship, the Dynatrope, were composed. It proved vulnerable to sulphuric acid.

THE KROTONS
See also *Dynatrope, Krotons*

TEMMOSUS

This scrupulous and over-trusting Thal leader was killed by the Daleks and succeeded by Alydon.

THE DEAD PLANET
See also *Alydon*

TERILEPTILS

An intelligent, technologically advanced reptilian race who, when encountered by the Doctor, were stranded on Earth in 1666. Fugitives from the prison planet Raaga, they attempted to destroy humanity with a virulent strain of plague, preparatory to colonisation of Earth. The Doctor tracked them down to a bakery in Pudding Lane where a fight ensued which killed the three Terileptils and ignited the Great Fire of London.

THE VISITATION
See also *Mace, Raaga*

TERMINUS

A hospital ship situated at the centre of the

universe, housing the victims of the highly contagious Lazars' disease. It was incompetently run by the Vanir, employees of a corrupt company, and the Garm who treated the sufferers in the irradiated Forbidden Zone. The Doctor discovered that Terminus, originally piloted by giant aliens, had unwittingly precipitated the creation of the universe by ejecting fuel into a void. Projected millions of years into the future by the ensuing blast, Terminus was on the point of repeating its error until stabilised by the Doctor and the Garm.

TERMINUS
See also *Garm, Lazars' Disease, Vanir*

TESH
Sworn enemies of the Sevateem, their ancestors had been technicians of an Earth spaceship from which both feuding tribes were descended. The Tesh had remained in the ship, serving Xoanon, suppressing their emotions and developing mind control and telepathy.

THE FACE OF EVIL
See also *Sevateem, Xoanon*

THALIRA
King Peladon's daughter and Queen of Peladon whom the Doctor met on his second trip to that planet. He helped the Queen to appease the rebellious miners and defeat Eckersley and the invading Ice Warriors.

THE MONSTER OF PELADON
See also *Eckersley, Ice Warriors, Peladon*

THALS
A race of blonde-haired humanoids who inhabited the planet Skaro. Their interminable war of attrition with their fellow natives, the Kaleds, precipitated the development of the Daleks who virtually annihilated the Thals. The survivors became pacifists, developing anti-radiation drugs which enabled them to inhabit the planet's surface until, once more they were compelled to fight for their lives against their hereditary enemies. Resigned to the impossibility of peace whilst the Daleks survived, the

Thals became their hunters. The Doctor encountered a Thal party on Spiridon, where he helped to disable a force of 10,000 Daleks.

THE DEAD PLANET – GENESIS OF THE DALEKS
See also *Daleks, Kaleds, Skaro*

THARILS
The furry lion-faced Tharils had once ruled an oppressive empire which was eventually overthrown by Gundan robots. They were time sensitives, able to ride the time winds and select a probable future occurrence and visualise until it became reality. This talent made them invaluable time-navigators and the Tharils encountered by the Doctor in E-Space were escaped slaves who had been forced to navigate Rorvik's spaceship. Romana and K9 left the Doctor to travel with the Tharils through the Warriors' Gate into an alternative universe.

WARRIORS' GATE
See also *Rorvik, Warriors' Gate*

THAWN
The corrupt controller of the methane refinery on Delta Three. Having bribed Rohm Dutt to incite a Swampie attack on the refinery, an act which was supposed to result in their mass murder, he was speared through the heart by one of his intended victims.

THE POWER OF KROLL
See also *Kroll, Swampies*

THINK TANK
A restricted scientific research centre which secretly housed the Giant Robot. Miss Winters, the malicious director and many of the employees belonged to the Scientific Reform Society which aimed to restructure the world on rational and scientific lines.

ROBOT
See *Winters*

TIBETAN MONKS
The normally peaceful monks of the Det-Sen monastery had developed a small warrior sect to protect themselves from the Yeti who were, unbeknown to them, controlled by their possessed master Padmasambhava.

THE ABOMINABLE SNOWMEN
See also *Padmasambhava, Yeti*

TIGELLA
An overgrown jungle planet whose inhabitants lived in an underground city powered by the Dodecahedron. Following the destruction of this artefact on Tigella's sister planet Zolpha-Thura, the Tigellans emerged to reclaim the planet's surface from the hostile vegetation.

MEGLOS
See also *Deons, Dodecahedron, Savants*

TIGUS
A volcanic planet upon which the Doctor was betrayed by the Meddling Monk to the Daleks.

THE DALEK MASTER PLAN
See also *Meddling Monk*

TIMANOV
Timanov was a dedicated elder of Logar clinging to antiquated legends amidst

growing sceptism. Having failed to convince Malkon of the validity of ritual burning he turned to the Master to endorse his beliefs. Timanov declined evacuation with his people, immolating himself instead in the fire of his mountain god.

PLANET OF FIRE
See also *Logar, Malkon Sarn*

TIME DESTRUCTOR
A terrifying weapon of the Daleks. Its vital element, the Taranium Core, was stolen by the Doctor and used to destroy them. Sara Kingdom, accidentally trapped within range of the Destructor, also perished.

THE DALEK MASTER PLAN
See also *Sara Kingdom*

TIME LORDS
The Time Lords are an immensely powerful, though somewhat stagnant race of the planet Gallifrey who have mastered time travel. They are mildly telepathic and possess two hearts, a respiratory bypass system, an average temperature of 60° Fahrenheit, and can regenerate their bodies twelve times, thus enabling them to live to phenomenal ages. Time Lord society, which is intensely structured and hierarchical is governed by the High Council who are elected from the noble chapters of Gallifrey, the most famous of which include the Arcalians, Patrexes and Prydonians. At the head of the High Council is the President, most powerful of his race who, on retirement, selects his own successor. Having graduated from the Academy, a Time Lord is expected to assume a predetermined role in the running of the Capitol, the main function of which is to monitor space-time events and record them in the Matrix.

Not surprisingly, several Time Lords have rejected the structures of Capitol life, absconding, usually in TARDISes, to become renegade travellers. Their numbers include the Doctor, the Master, Morbius, the Meddling Monk, Drax, the War Chief, Salyavin, Nesbin and Romana. Following the Time Lords' disastrous interference in the history of the planet Minyos, they adopted a non-intervention policy of pure observation which was later modified by the Doctor's humanitarian plea at his trial. Since then the Time Lords, in particular the CIA (Celestial Intervention Agency) have taken a more positive interest in events, frequently involving the Doctor, former President of the Time Lords, as an unwilling emissary.

See also *Borusa, Doctor, Gallifrey, Master, Matrix, Omega, Prydonians, Rassilon, Romana, Shobogans*

TIME RING
A preprogrammed bracelet presented to the Doctor by the Time Lords, which transported his companions and himself from Skaro to Nerva Beacon. To the dismay of Harry Sullivan, it disintegrated on arrival on the Beacon.

GENESIS OF THE DALEKS
REVENGE OF THE CYBERMEN

TIME SCANNER
This machine, the invention of Professor Fendelman, projected images of Earth's past, locating and activating the skull housing the Fendahl. Converted into a

time bomb by the Doctor it imploded, destroying Fetch Priory and the Fendahl.

THE IMAGE OF THE FENDAHL
See also *Fendahl, Fendelman*

TIME SCOOP
As a precursor to Operation Golden Age, Professor Whitaker's time machine transported Dinosaurs to twentieth century London from Earth's prehistoric past. He and his confederate Grover were mistakenly projected back in time with them.

INVASION OF THE DINOSAURS
See also *Operation Golden Age*

TIME-SPACE VISUALISER
This time television, a former exhibit in the Space Museum, was presented to the Doctor by the Xerons. Tuning to the appropriate dates and locations, the TARDIS crew viewed Abraham Lincoln, William Shakespeare, and the Beatles. Left to its own devices the image revealed a Dalek fleet leaving Skaro, its purpose to find and exterminate the Doctor.

THE SPACE MUSEUM
THE CHASE

TITAN
The largest of Saturn's ten moons housed a refuelling base which was contacted and invaded by the Nucleus of the Swarm. The Titan asteroid was destroyed by the Doctor, killing the Nucleus and its newly-spawned Swarm.

THE INVISIBLE ENEMY
See also *Nucleus*

TLOTOXL
The devious High Priest of Sacrifice who thwarted Barbara's attempt to eradicate human sacrifice from his Aztec culture.

THE AZTECS
See also *Yetaxa*

T-MAT

The T-MAT or Transmat is a form of instantaneous travel between two fixed locations. A Moon to Earth T-Mat was intercepted by the Ice Warriors in the twenty-first century and used by them to project deadly seed pods to Earth. The Doctor repaired another version enabling the newly-revived inhabitants of Nerva Beacon to return to Earth. An earlier journey in the same machine cured Sarah of the Cyber virus by separating her molecules from the poison.

THE SEEDS OF DEATH
THE ARK IN SPACE
REVENGE OF THE CYBERMEN

TOBA

The more sadistic of the two Dominators controlling Dulkis. He perished with his superior Rago in the explosion of the Dominator ship.

THE DOMINATORS
See also *Dominators*

TODD

The intelligent and open-minded science officer of the survey team on Deva Loka. She sensed the hidden powers and knowledge of the apparently primitive Kinda and strongly disapproved of her superior's repressive tactics towards them.

KINDA
See also *Hindle, Sanders*

TOM-TIT

Transmission Of Matter Through Interstitial Time: a time-disrupting machine created by the Master to transport Kronos to Earth. In his battle against UNIT he also summoned medieval knights, Roundheads and a flying bomb and regressed Sergeant Benton to babyhood, from which he recovered with the eventual destruction of the machine.

THE TIME MONSTER
See also *Kronos*

TRACTATORS

The Tractators resemble huge scaly upright caterpillars and are by nature passive burrowing creatures. Once controlled by the Gravis however their collective magnetic powers attracted showers of destructive meteorites to Frontios and dragged colonists beneath the earth to a gruesome fate. With the Gravis removed the Tractators resumed their docile subterranean activities.

FRONTIOS
See also *Frontios, Gravis, Trion*

TRAKEN, UNION OF

A union of planets maintained in a perpetual state of peace and harmony by its union with the Bio-Electronic Source, a power so intense that evil immediately calcifies within its influence. The peace of Traken was shattered by the Master's plot to become Keeper of Traken, merging with the Source to tap its awsome powers and regenerate himself. It was the Master's subsequent interference in the computations of Logopolis which sealed the fate of this inoffensive planet, which was engulfed and obliterated in the ensuing tide of entropy.

THE KEEPER OF TRAKEN
LOGOPOLIS
See also *Melkur, Nyssa, Tremas*

TRAVERS, PROFESSOR EDWARD

An abrupt and fanatical explorer who eventually became the Doctor's friend, having initially accused him of murder whilst investigating the legends of the Yeti in the Himalayas. Over forty years later, Travers, now an old professor with an adult daughter, Anne, was reunited with Jamie, Victoria and the Doctor and helped them to defeat the reactivated Yeti menacing the London Underground.

THE ABOMINABLE SNOWMEN
THE WEB OF FEAR
See also *Great Intelligence, Yeti*

TREMAS

This altruistic and aristocratic Consul of Traken was chosen by the dying Keeper of Traken to become his successor. The exalted and dedicated post would inevitably isolate Tremas from Nyssa his daughter, and Kassia his new wife. Kassia's intrigues to retain her husband resulted in his imprisonment and eventual death at the hands of the Master who also stole his body.

THE KEEPER OF TRAKEN
See also *Kassia, Master, Nyssa, Traken*

TRENCHARD

The credulous governor of the prison on Earth holding the Master who helped the convicted criminal to raid a naval base. Eventually recognising his own stupidity Trenchard revolted and was immediately killed by the Sea Devils.

THE SEA DEVILS
See also *Sea Devils*

TRILOGIC GAME

The Celestial Toymaker's ultimate game involving verbally controlled building blocks from which the Doctor was to construct a pyramid. The Doctor outmanoeuvred the Toymaker by impersonating his adversary's voice on the final move, thus enabling the TARDIS to escape the ensuing destruction of the magician's world.

THE CELESTIAL TOYMAKER
See also *Celestial Toymaker*

TRION

A technologically sophisticated civilisation, governed by autocratic imperial clans, was to be found on Trion. When civil war erupted deposing the hierarchical regime many former luminaries, including Turlough's family, were branded with the Trion convict mark (the Misos triangle) and deported to the prison planet Sarn. Turlough, his brother and numerous descendants of Trion prisoners were eventually readmitted by the tolerant new order. An ancestral memory buried in Turlough's subconscious suggests that Trion was once plagued by Tractators.

PLANET OF FIRE
See also *Sarn, Tractators, Turlough*

TRISILICATE

A valuable mineral mined on Peladon, which proved essential to the Federation's war effort against Galaxy Five. It was also desired by the Ice Warriors.

THE CURSE OF PELADON
THE MONSTER OF PELADON
See also *Galaxy Five, Ice Warriors, Peladon*

TROGS

The descendants of the Minyans aboard the crashed P7E, who, oppressed for generations by the Oracle and its servants the Seers, endured a miserable subterranean existence until rescued by Jackson and his crew.

THE UNDERWORLD
See also *Jackson, Oracle, P7E*

TROILUS

Adopting the name Cressida, Vicki left the TARDIS to stay with the Trojan Prince Troilus, a survivor of the massacre of Troy, with whom she had fallen in love.

THE MYTH MAKERS
See also *Troy, Vicki*

TROY

The virtually impregnable city of the Trojans which withstood the onslaughts of a combined Grecian army for ten years. The Doctor, coerced by Odysseus, invented the wooden horse which brought about the eventual downfall of the city.

THE MYTH MAKERS

TRYST

This interplanetory zoologist and inventor of the CET machine, secretly used his invention to smuggle the drug vraxoin. The Doctor apprehended the escaping criminal with the CET machine.

NIGHTMARE OF EDEN
See also *Vraxoin*

T.S.S.

The Total Survival Suit was a sophisticated though cumbersome exploration machine brought to Deva Loka by Sanders' expeditionary force. Functioning through a telepathic link with the brainwaves of the occupant, the machine went out of control when stolen by a confused and frightened Adric.

KINDA

TURLOUGH, VISLOR

Posing as a public schoolboy at the institution attended by former Brigadier, now teacher, Lethbridge-Stewart, was Turlough, who became one of the Doctor's most amoral and enigmatic companions. An alien stranded on Earth, he was recruited by the Black Guardian to kill the Doctor in exchange for his freedom, but in his subsequent travels in the TARDIS the self-centred alien found himself eventually siding with the Doctor against his former master.

Following the discovery of his younger brother Malkon on the erupting planet Sarn, Turlough finally revealed his origins as a native of the planet Trion from which he and his family had been exiled. Having summoned a Trion spaceship to evacuate the population, Turlough and Malkon returned home, their exile revoked.

MAWDRYN UNDEAD – PLANET OF FIRE
See also *Guardian, Black, Malkon, Sarn, Trion*

TYSSAN

A former terrestrial spaceman Tyssan endured two years of underground captivity slaving for the Daleks on Skaro, before escaping to help the Doctor defeat the Movellans, the Daleks and the reanimated Davros. He and his fellow slaves left for Earth in a Movellan ship bearing the frozen Davros.

DESTINY OF THE DALEKS
See also *Daleks, Davros, Movellans*

TYTHONUS

A planet rich in minerals but bereft of chlorophyll essential to the diet of the huge green Tythonians. The Tythonians, who live for about 40,000 years, communicate and ingest their food through the skin and, although peaceful and sedentary by nature, were able to harness the power of neutron stars, making them capable of destroying whole star systems. The Doctor persuaded Erato to deflect one such star which had been launched at Chloris in retribution for the unlawful imprisonment of Erato, the Tythonian ambassador by the Lady Adrasta.

THE CREATURE FROM THE PIT
See also *Adrasta, Erato, Chloris*

UNIT

The United Nations Intelligence Taskforce, a military organisation with its headquarters in Geneva, was established to counter alien menaces to the Earth. It evolved from the suggestions and observations of one Colonel Lethbridge-Stewart following his involvement with the invasion of London's Underground by the Yeti.

UNIT's first action involved the Cybermen then, coinciding with the arrival of the exiled third Doctor, the British branch of UNIT commanded by Brigadier Lethbridge-Stewart became deluged by potentially hostile extra-terrestials, all planning to invade the Earth. Those encountered included the Nestenes, Silurians, peaceful alien ambassadors, the Master, Axos, the Daemons, Daleks, Ogrons, Sea Devils, Kronos, Omega, Zygons, Androids and Krynoids, not to mention such home-grown perils as the Primords, Giant Maggots, Dinosaurs and the Giant Robot. Besides the Brigadier, regular members of UNIT have included Captain Yates, Benton, Liz Shaw, Jo Grant and Lieutenant Harry Sullivan.

THE WEB OF FEAR – THE ANDROID INVASION
See also *Brigadier, Harry Sullivan, Jo Grant, Liz Shaw, Yates*

URBANKANS

Green frog-like beings whose planet Urbanka was destroyed by Monarch's experiments which eroded the ozone

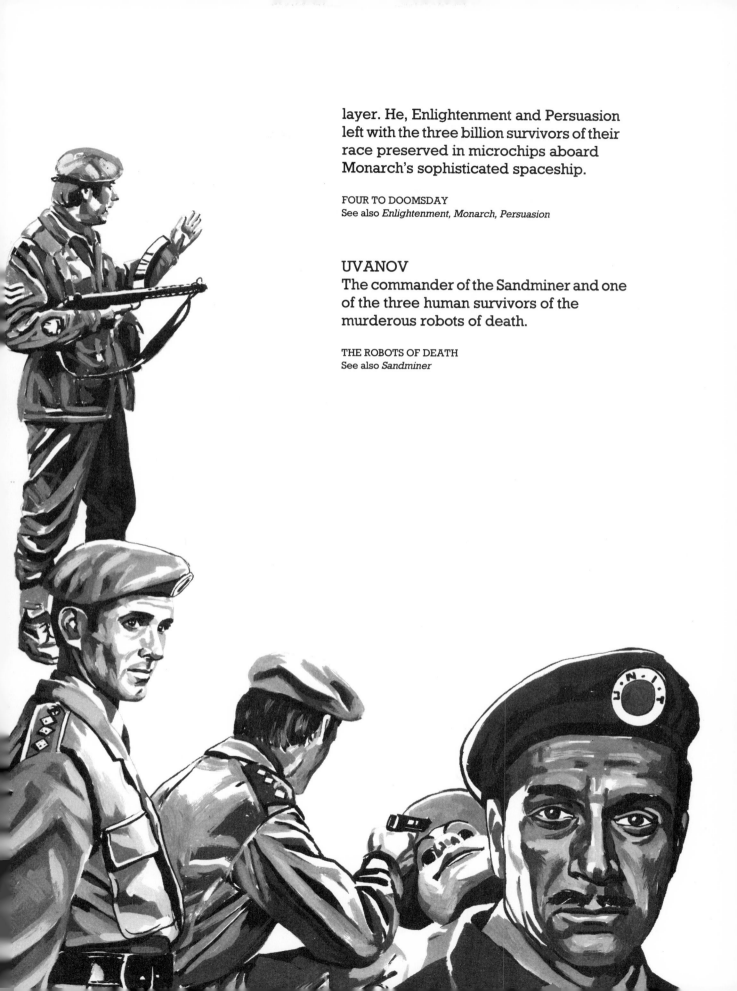

layer. He, Enlightenment and Persuasion left with the three billion survivors of their race preserved in microchips aboard Monarch's sophisticated spaceship.

FOUR TO DOOMSDAY
See also *Enlightenment, Monarch, Persuasion*

UVANOV
The commander of the Sandminer and one of the three human survivors of the murderous robots of death.

THE ROBOTS OF DEATH
See also *Sandminer*

V

VAAGA PLANTS
A particularly hostile form of plant life from the planet Skaro which accompanied the Daleks to Kembel, infecting Marc Cory's two shipmates. A prick from the poisonous Vaaga thorn produces a creeping white furry coating of the victim's flesh, violent insanity and ultimately metamorphosis into a Vaaga Plant.

MISSION TO THE UNKNOWN
See also *Cory, Kembel*

VALGARD
A tough, disillusioned, though basically just member of the Vanir who eventually deposed his corrupt superior and, with the Doctor's advice and Nyssa's aid, prepared to reform Terminus.

TERMINUS
See also *Terminus, Vanir*

VAMPIRES
An immensely powerful blood-sucking race who swarmed over the galaxy, draining planets of life. All but one perished in a bloody battle with the Time Lords who, under the command of Rassilon, developed bow ships the metal projectiles of which pierced the hearts of the monsters, killing them.

STATE OF DECAY
See also *Great Vampire, Rassilon*

VANIR
The custodians and guards of Terminus, whose fearsome armoured attire concealed weary drug-dependent humans, employed by a corrupt company to handle the Lazars. Faring little better than their diseased charges, inadequately protected by their armour from the irradiated environment and supplied with insufficient doses of hydromel, they discharged their duties with cultivated detachment. Nyssa's ability to synthesise adequate amounts of hydromel aboard Terminus ended their dependence on the company, thus enabling them to devote their energies to the investigation and cure of Lazars' disease.

TERMINUS
See also *Hydromel, Terminus, Valgard*

VARAN
A Solonian warchief and hereditary enemy of Ky. He supported the Overlord regime until his son was deceitfully murdered by the Marshal. The distraught and rapidly mutating warchief led his warriors in a suicide attack on Skybase where they were exterminated by the Marshal.

THE MUTANTS
See also *Ky, Marshal, Skybase, Solos*

VARDANS
Alien humanoids possessing the capacity to read minds and travel and materialise along wavelengths. The Doctor, via a devious deception which endangered the security of Gallifrey, pin-pointed and time-looped their home planet, disposing of the

Vardan menace to Gallifrey, but precipitating the invasion of the Sontarans, who had used the Vardans as their bridgehead.

THE INVASION OF TIME
See also *Sontarans*

VARGA
A ruthless Ice Warrior warlord, the commander of a Martian spaceship dispatched to reconnoitre Earth, which crashed during the First Ice Age – remaining preserved for centuries until Varga's frozen body was discovered during the Second Ice Age. The reanimated warlord revitalised his crew, but both he and his Ice Warriors ultimately fell victim to the heat of the ioniser, perishing in the explosion of their ship as they attempted to blast out of the ice.

THE ICE WARRIORS
See also *Ice Warriors*

VARSH
Adric's adored elder brother, a rebellious non-conformist, rejected the strictures of the Starliner to lead a small band of juveniles, the Outlers. Finally perceiving the dangers of Mistfall, he returned to fight the Marshmen aboard the Starliner, dying heroically before the eyes of his stunned brother.

FULL CIRCLE
See also *Adric, Outlers, Starliner*

VAUGHN, TOBIAS
The deviously charming director of International Electromatix who, seduced by promises of universal power, proved instrumental in the Cyberman invasion of Earth. Vaughn eventually united with the Doctor to defeat his former allies who killed him.

THE INVASION
See also *Cerebration Mentor, International Electromatix*

VEGA NEXOS
A mole-man mining engineer of the planet Vega and an innocent colleague of Eckersley. He was killed by the manifestation of Aggedor.

THE MONSTER OF PELADON
See also *Aggedor, Eckersley, Peladon*

VENOM GRUBS
A species of unsavoury death-spitting centipede, manipulated as weapons by the Animus-possessed Zarbi.

THE WEB PLANET
See also *Animus, Vortis, Zarbi*

VENUSIAN AIKIDO
A form of unarmed combat perfected by the six-armed Venusians (of whose lullabies the Doctor was particularly fond). The third Doctor took great pride in his mastery of this extremely complex martial art.

VICKI
When the Earth ship carrying Vicki and her father to the planet Astra crashed on Dido, she and Bennett were the sole survivors. Bennett had, unbeknown to the trusting girl, murdered the other crew

members. Missing his recently-departed granddaughter, the Doctor readily welcomed the orphaned girl aboard the TARDIS.

The quiet intelligent teenager remained with the Doctor following the departure of Barbara and Ian, and was accompanied for a while by Steven Taylor. Vicki eventually bade the TARDIS a tearful farewell on the plains of Troy where, having adopted the Trojan name Cressida, she left to begin a new life with Prince Troilus.

THE RESCUE – THE MYTH MAKERS
See also *Bennett, Troilus*

VICTORIA WATERFIELD
A demure, kindly Victorian girl whose father, Edward Waterfield, had invented a time machine, drawing him to the attention of the Daleks who kidnapped Victoria to ensure his co-operation in their scheme to trap the Doctor. The dying Waterfield made the Doctor his daughter's guardian, a responsibility happily shared by Jamie who proved immensely protective towards the sensitive girl. Victoria gradually adapted to TARDIS life adopting more serviceable and adventurous attire whilst retaining a consistent terror of anything alien. Her predilection for screaming at hostile life forms destroyed the noise-sensitive weed creatures which were menacing a gas exploration rig where Victoria, never a wanderer by nature, accepted a stable home with the Harris family on the refinery.

EVIL OF THE DALEKS – FURY FROM THE DEEP
See also *Jamie, Waterfield, Weed Creatures*

VIRA
The first Medtech aboard Space Ark Nerva, who was revived from cryogenic suspension having overslept by thousands of years. Although initially detached and suspicious of the time travellers, she helped them defeat the Wirrn, taking command when her prospective mate, Noah, mutated into a giant insect. The Doctor repaired the Transmat, enabling Vira to transport her people to Earth.

THE ARK IN SPACE
See also *Nerva Beacon, Noah*

VISHINSKY
A veteran space traveller, second in command to the incompetent Salamar aboard the Morestran probe ship. Eventually compelled to assume command, he saved both his ship and the life of the Doctor.

PLANET OF EVIL
See also *Zeta Minor*

VISIANS
Giant, vicious, invisible creatures of the

110

planet Mira, they trapped the Doctor and his friends inside a cave when the time travellers were attempting to elude the Daleks.

THE DALEK MASTER PLAN

VOCS
Sophisticated vocal robots aboard the Sandminer, the two other classifications being the menial Dums and the versatile Super-Vocs.

THE ROBOTS OF DEATH
See also *SV7*

VOGA
Voga, the mythical Planet of Gold and once a major power, was virtually destroyed in the first Cyber war. A fragment of Voga survived, however, its existence anathema to the gold-sensitive Cybermen who desired its total destruction. The Cybermen, having relocated the lost fragment, attempted by

means of human-transported bomb packs and the bomb-laden Nerva Beacon to finally erradicate their ancient enemies, but failed due to the last-minute intervention by the Doctor.

REVENGE OF THE CYBERMEN
See also *Cybermen, Vogans*

VOGANS
The large-eyed, dome-headed inhabitants of Voga adopted a subterranean existence following the devastation of their planet by the Cybermen. Led by Councillor Tyrum they kept their survival secret until the fanatical Vorus used Kellman to attract the attention of the Cybermen, planning to lure them to destruction on Nerva Beacon.

REVENGE OF THE CYBERMEN
See also *Voga, Vorus*

VOORD
Vicious featureless creatures clad in acid-resistant suits who, having developed a resistance to the Conscience of Marinus, invaded the pyramid housing the machine, killing Arbitan in their quest to possess the keys.

THE KEYS OF MARINUS
See also *Arbitan, Conscience of Marinus, Yartek*

VORG
An optimistic galactic showman who landed on Inter Minor with his assistant Shirna and his precious Scope, to entertain the poker-faced inhabitants.

CARNIVAL OF MONSTERS
See also *Scope*

111

VORSHAK
The beleaguered commander of Sea Base Four faced internal sabotage plus the joint threat of Sea Devils and Silurians. A fierce battle ensued, culminating in the futile deaths of all involved, the final victim being Vorshak himself.

WARRIORS OF THE DEEP
See also *Sea Base Four, Sea Devils, Silurians*

VORTIS
A silent, rocky, inhospitable planet once ruled by the benign Menoptera with their passive Zarbi servants. The malign influence of the Animus enveloped Vortis in a creeping web, controlling the now-hostile Zarbi and exerting a magnetic force which drew the helpless TARDIS to the planet.

THE WEB PLANET
See also *Animus, Menoptera, Zarbi*

VORUS
An arrogant, ambitious Vogan who, with the aid of the scientist Magrik, constructed the Skystriker rocket to fulfil his ultimate dream; the destruction of the Cybermen. Vorus was killed by Tyrum whilst igniting his rocket which would have destroyed Nerva Beacon had not the Doctor redirected it to the Cyberman spaceship.

REVENGE OF THE CYBERMEN
See also *Voga*

VRAXOIN
The most addictive drug in the galaxy, composed from decomposed Mandrels. It was smuggled by Tryst in the Eden projection of his CET machine.

NIGHTMARE OF EDEN
See also *Mandrels*

VRESTIN
The leader of the ill-fated Menoptera invasion force, who befriended Ian whilst escaping from the Zarbi. Vrestin persuaded the subterranean Optera to burrow to the surface and attack the Animus.

THE WEB PLANET
See also *Animus, Menoptera, Optera, Zarbi*

VULCAN
An Earth colony where three deactivated Daleks were discovered and reanimated with disastrous repercussions.

THE POWER OF THE DALEKS
See also *Lesterson*

VYON, BRET
This dedicated space security agent allied himself with the Doctor on Kembel to defeat the invading Daleks. Having escaped in a stolen spaceship, Bret was shot by his sister, Sara Kingdom.

THE DALEK MASTER PLAN
See also *Sara Kingdom*

WAR CHIEF
An unprincipled renegade Time Lord who constructed Sidrats for use in the War Games in exchange for promises of power. The Doctor's interference implicated the War Chief in deception as a result of which he was shot whilst attempting to escape in a Sidrat.

THE WAR GAMES
See also *Sidrats, War Games, War Lord*

WAR GAMES
A series of battles fought on an alien planet between Earth soldiers, uprooted from a particular war, processed, and transported without their knowledge. Each War Zone, from the Roman period to the Great War, was supervised by alien commanders whose hypnotic powers perpetuated the deception in the minds of the majority of the participants. The ultimate aim of the Games was to compile an invincible fighting force.

THE WAR GAMES
See also *War Chief, War Lord*

WAR LORD
The pitiless leader of the alien race who instigated the War Games. Having destroyed the War Chief, he was eventually captured by the Time Lords and sentenced to dematerialisation.

THE WAR GAMES
See *War Chief, War Games*

WAR MACHINES
Fully-armed mobile computers resembling miniature tanks which were constructed on the instructions of WOTAN. The Doctor reprogrammed one to destroy its creator and deactivated the remainder.

THE WAR MACHINES
See also *Wotan*

WARRIORS' GATE
A mirrored archway forming an interface between E-Space and Normal Space, it dated from the Great Empire of the Tharils who used it to return home. Its selective entry restored damaged body tissue and enabled the Tharils to travel through Time and Space. The Doctor, K9 and Romana passed through the mirrors, the latter deciding to remain in E-Space with the Tharils and K9 whose mechanical constitution precluded a return trip through the Gate.

WARRIORS' GATE
See also *E-Space, Tharils*

WATCHER
The Doctor's alternative body who mysteriously appeared just prior to his fourth regeneration, rescuing Nyssa from Traken and piloting the TARDIS from Logopolis to Earth. Following the fourth Doctor's crippling fall from the radio telescope at the Pharos Project, the Watcher merged with his dying body, regenerating into the fifth Doctor.

LOGOPOLIS
See also *Pharos Project*

WATERFIELD, PROFESSOR EDWARD

Victoria's father, having co-invented a time machine, was coerced by threats to his daughter's life to co-operate with the Daleks. Waterfield perished in an act of self-sacrifice, saving the Doctor's life on Skaro.

EVIL OF THE DALEKS
See also *Victoria*

WATKINS, PROFESSOR AND ISOBEL

The Doctor encountered Isobel, the photographer niece of Professor Watkins, whilst paying an impromptu visit to the home of his old friend Professor Travers. Watkins had disappeared, a prisoner of Tobias Vaughn who forced him to modify the Cerebration Mentor for use against the Cybermen. With the aid of his niece, the professor was rescued and the Cybermen invasion defeated.

THE INVASION
See also *Cerebration Mentor, Travers, Vaughn*

WEED CREATURES

Massive parasitic seaweed creatures who, activated by off-shore drilling operations, emerged from the North Sea, attacking a refinery by infecting and mutating its inhabitants. Through Victoria's screams, the Doctor perceived the Weed's intolerance to high frequency sound waves and disposed of the creatures.

FURY FROM THE DEEP

WENG-CHIANG

Magnus Greel, alias Weng-Chiang (a Chinese god whom he impersonated whilst stranded in nineteenth century China) was a murderous war criminal who escaped from the fifty-first century with his evil creation Mr Sin. The Zygma time experiments which transported him to the nineteenth century infected him with a crippling disease, only temporarily

alleviated by the distillation and transference of the life source of young women. Having discovered his lost Time Cabinet in Victorian England he was subjected to total cellular collapse whilst attempting to reactivate it.

THE TALONS OF WENG-CHIANG
See also *Sin*

WHEEL
Space Station W3 LX88J (the Wheel) which deflected meteorites from one of Earth's valuable space trade routes was invaded by Cybermats and Cybermen, as a prelude to an attempted conquest of Earth. The Doctor disposed of the Cybermen with the aid of Wheel crew member Zoe Herriot.

THE WHEEL IN SPACE
See also *Zoe*

WHITAKER, PROFESSOR
The inventor of the Time Scoop which instigated Operation Golden Age. He, and his confederate Grover were eventually transported back to Earth's prehistory by the Scoop.

INVASION OF THE DINOSAURS
See also *Operation Golden Age, Time Scoop*

WHOMOBILE
A futuristic streamlined silver vehicle designed by the third Doctor. Resembling a cross between a racing car and a hovercraft, this jet-propelled vehicle was also capable of flight.

PLANET OF THE SPIDERS

WILL CHANDLER
This survivor of the 1643 massacre of Little Hodcombe was accidentally projected to 1984 by the energy of the Malus. The confused adolescent helped the Doctor prevent a re-enactment of the massacre.

THE AWAKENING
See also *Malus*

WIND CHIMES
A tinkling structure of dangling crystal beneath which the telepathic Kinda shared meditations.

KINDA
See also *Dukkha*

WINTERS, HILDA
The unethical director of Think Tank who used the Giant Robot and her dictatorial influence over her gullible fellow scientists to gain access to an experimental atomic bomb shelter. From the safety of the bunker she prepared to initiate a nuclear war upon the rejection of her demands for world domination. The Doctor prevented the catastrophe, Miss Winters having surrendered to a gun-wielding Sarah Jane Smith.

ROBOT
See also *Think Tank*

WIRRN
A parasitic breed of intelligent man-sized insect resembling wasps who exist in Space, occasionally landing in search of food and breeding facilities. With that intent the Wirrn Queen penetrated Nerva Beacon, laying her eggs in one of the

sleeping humans, who nurtured the suppurating larvae within Nerva's solar chambers. The overwhelming hordes of hatching Wirrn were diverted to their doom by Noah.

THE ARK IN SPACE
See also *Nerva, Noah*

WOLF WEEDS
The vicious carnivorous tumbleweed pets of Lady Adrasta. These anti-social mobile bushes attacked K9 and were eventually eaten by the vegetarian Erato.

THE CREATURE FROM THE PIT
See also *Adrasta, Erato*

WORLD ECOLOGY BUREAU
An international organisation which contacted the Doctor to identify the mysterious Krynoid pods. One of the bureau's employees, Dunbar, disclosed classified information on the pods to Harrison Chase.

THE SEEDS OF DOOM
See also *Chase, Krynoid*

WOTAN
The Will-Operating Thought Analogue (WOTAN for short) was the ultimate self-reasoning computer, built by Professor Brett and housed in the newly-constructed Post Office Tower. Having brainwashed his creator, the machine gained control over Polly, Dodo and numerous other humans whom he hypnotised by telephone. WOTAN sought world domination by linking programs with computers world-wide. To suppress opposition it had constructed the War Machines, one of which eventually destroyed it.

THE WAR MACHINES
See also *War Machines*

WRACK
The decadently devious captain of the pirate ship *Buccaneer* who collaborated with the Black Guardian, gleefully plotting the demise of her fellow Eternals whilst competing in a bizarre space race.

ENLIGHTENMENT
See also *Guardian, Black, Eternals*

The Time Lords of Gallifrey.

The TARDIS – gateway to time and space.

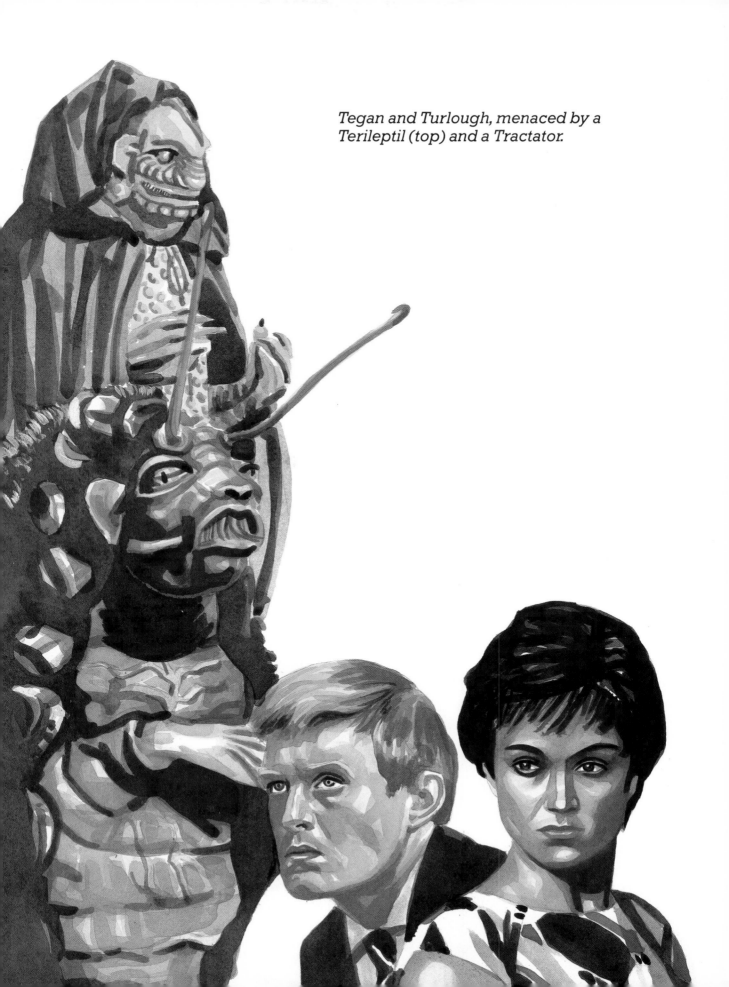

Tegan and Turlough, menaced by a Terileptil (top) and a Tractator.

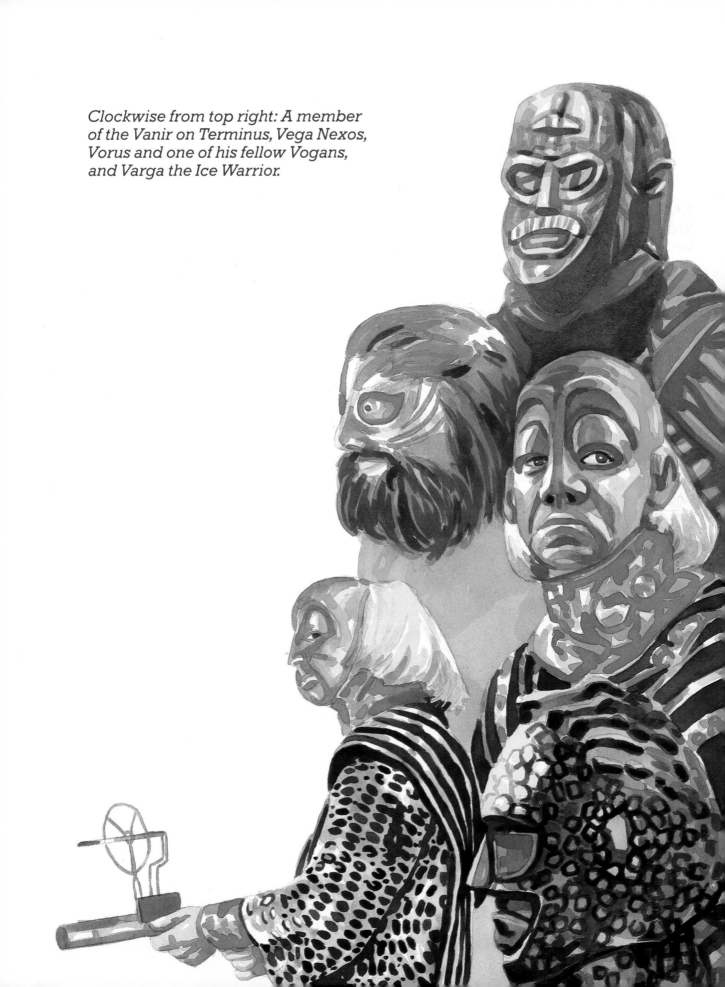

Clockwise from top right: A member of the Vanir on Terminus, Vega Nexos, Vorus and one of his fellow Vogans, and Varga the Ice Warrior.

XANXIA

The evil wizened queen of Zanak, believed to be long dead, wielded the power behind the Pirate Captain, sucking planets dry to reanimate her decaying body. The re-embodied Xanxia, having killed the rebellious captain, perished herself when disconnected from her energy supply.

THE PIRATE PLANET

XERAPHIN

A highly advanced life form of the planet Xeriphas possessing awesome psychic and psychokinetic powers, who migrated to Earth, their own planet having been devastated in an alien war. To recover from the radiation sickness which had infected them, the entire Xeraphin race bonded into one bioplasmic entity housed within a sarcophagus in their citadel on Earth. There they were discovered by the Master who tapped the dark side of their psychic energy, creating the Plasmatons and eventually stealing the sarcophagus which, through the Doctor's intervention, was ultimately returned with the Master to a radiation-free Xeriphas.

TIME-FLIGHT
See also *Plasmatons*

XOANON

The fourth Doctor hastily repaired this experimental sentient computer belonging to an Earth colony. It subsequently retained traces of his personality, voice and image, and developed schizophrenia. The disturbed machine perpetuated its mental confusion in the Earth colonists, dividing them into two incompatible tribes: the Tesh, obsessed with mental perfection, and the Sevateem, reliant on physical powers, each worshipping Xoanon as a god. The Doctor eventually returned, remedying his mistake and returning the grateful computer to sanity.

THE FACE OF EVIL
See also *Sevateem, Tesh*

YARTEK
The villainous leader of the Voord who destroyed himself, the Voord and the Conscience of Marinus by inserting a false key into the machine.

THE KEYS OF MARINUS
See also *Conscience, Voord*

YATES, CAPTAIN MIKE
The intelligent and sensitive subordinate of the Brigadier whose courage and leadership proved instrumental in the defeat of several alien invasions. Having been brainwashed by BOSS, the confused Yates was given extended leave, returning to UNIT during the dinosaur invasion in which he was revealed to be heavily implicated with the enemy. The young captain was subsequently invalided out of the army. Yates retired to a meditation centre to recover from his traumatic experiences and, whilst there, alerted Sarah and the Doctor to the menace of the Metebelis Spiders, whom he helped to defeat.

TERROR OF THE AUTONS – PLANET OF THE SPIDERS
See also *BOSS, Whitaker*

YETAXA
Barbara was believed to be the reincarnation of the god Yetaxa, in whose temple she was discovered by the Aztecs.

THE AZTECS

YETI
The Yeti were huge fur-covered robots animated by the Great Intelligence via small metallic spheres inserted into the creatures' chests. The Doctor first encountered them in the Himalayas, and again in the London Underground where they wielded deadly web guns. On both occasions the Yeti were deactivated by the destruction of the central pyramid of spheres controlled by the Intelligence. The Doctor had one further fleeting tussle with a Yeti in the Death Zone on Gallifrey.

THE ABOMINABLE SNOWMEN
THE WEB OF FEAR
THE FIVE DOCTORS
See also *Great Intelligence*

Z

ZA

The leader of the tribe of Gum whose knowledge of the origins of fire died with his father. Having removed the threat to his authority posed by Kal, the cunning caveman intended to imprison the firemaking time travellers who had saved his life.

THE TRIBE OF GUM
See also *Kal*

ZANAK

A hollow planet equipped with massive engines, enabling it to leap across the galaxy, rematerialising around unfortunate planets whose mineral wealth it then absorbed. The Mentiads, discovering the source of their planet's wealth, destroyed the bridge which controlled the engines of Zanak.

THE PIRATE PLANET
See also *Captain, Mentiads, Xanxia*

ZARBI

These terrifying chirruping insects resembling giant ants were possessed by the Animus, for whom they guarded the enslaved Menoptera on Vortis. Following Barbara's destruction of the Animus, they resumed their normally docile existence.

THE WEB PLANET
See also *Animus, Menoptera, Venom Grubs, Vortis*

ZARGO

Formerly Captain Miles Sharkey of the *Hydrax*.

STATE OF DECAY
See also *Aukon, Hydrax*

ZAROFF, PROFESSOR

This brilliant but psychotic scientist vanished from Earth in 1950 having achieved fame for his work on undersea food sources. Zaroff had discovered Atlantis where he continued his experiments, creating the hapless fishpeople, and pursuing his ultimate insane ambition, the destruction of the Earth. He finally died, drowning as seawater plunged through a gap in the seabed, made by himself.

THE UNDERWATER MENACE
See also *Atlantis, Fishpeople*

ZASTOR

The respected leader of Tigella who tirelessly mediated between the Deons and Savants, the two irreconcilable factions of his society. Being an old friend of the Doctor, he sought his help over the decline of the Dodecahedron.

MEGLOS
See also *Tigella*

Z BOMB

A highly destructive nuclear weapon which Ben prevented from being dispatched to Mondas, an action which would have rebounded on its twin planet, Earth.

THE TENTH PLANET
See also *Mondas*

ZEOS
The twin planet of Atrios, against which it waged war, controlled by the Mentalis computer.

THE ARMAGEDDON FACTOR
See also *Atrios, Mentalis*

ZERO ROOM
A neutral environment aboard the TARDIS, isolated from external interferences, in which the fifth Doctor languished, recovering from his unstable fourth regeneration. The room was subsequently jettisoned to enable the TARDIS to escape from destruction in Event One but a Zero Cabinet was constructed from its remains in which the Doctor was transported to Castrovalva.

CASTROVALVA
See also *Castrovalva*

ZETA MINOR
A bizarre jungle planet on the brink of the Morestrans' known universe. The Morestran probe ship landed there in search of alternative energy sources. Upon the planet was a mysterious black pool which served as a gateway into the universe of anti-matter.

PLANET OF EVIL
See also *Anti-Matter Monster, Morestra*

ZOE HERRIOT
Zoe was a super-intelligent product of the parapsychic unit school on Earth, which trained her to function logically and then dispatched her to the Space Wheel as a librarian. Rebelling against her emotionless education, she stowed away in the TARDIS following the defeat of the Cybermen on the Wheel. 'The Doctor is almost as clever as I am,' she once consented, and indeed, her incredible encyclopaedic and photographic brain often proved invaluable during her travels with the Doctor. Following the latter's capture by the Time Lords, Zoe was returned to the Wheel, her experiences with Jamie and the Doctor (save for their original encounter) totally erased from her memory.

THE WHEEL IN SPACE – THE WAR GAMES
See also *Wheel*

ZOLFA-THURA
A barren sandy planet supporting the five screens built by Meglos to harness the destructive powers of the Dodecahedron. A war ensued over their usage, from which Meglos was the sole survivor. Eventually returning with the Dodecahedron, he inadvertently atomised himself and the planet.

MEGLOS
See also *Dodecahedron, Meglos*

ZYGONS
An alien race covered in sucker-like protuberances, whose semi-organic spaceship crashed into Loch Ness. They possessed a chameleon-like ability to adopt the form of their human prisoners. The Zygons planned to restructure the Earth prior to its full-scale colonisation by their wandering spaceships, but fell foul of the Doctor who destroyed them.

TERROR OF THE ZYGONS
See also *Broton, Loch Ness Monster*